The Wound of Love

CISTERCIAN STUDIES SERIES: NUMBER ONE HUNDRED FIFTY-SEVEN

The Wound of Love

A Carthusian Miscellany

Cistercian Publications
Kalamazoo, Michigan

First Published 1994 by
Darton Longman Todd Ltd
London
&
Cistercian Publications Inc
WMU Station
Kalamazoo, Michigan 49008

© 1994 St Hugh's Charterhouse, Horsham, West Sussex

ISBN 0 87907 757 3

The work of Cistercian Publications is made possible in part
by support from Western Michigan University to
The Institute of Cistercian Studies

Phototypeset by Intype, London
Printed and bound in Great Britain
at the University Press, Cambridge

Here is acquired that eye,
by whose serene gaze the Spouse
is wounded with love;
that eye, pure and clean, by which God is seen.

(Statutes of the Carthusian Order 1.6.16)

Acknowledgements

*Grateful acknowledgement is given
to the following people who assisted the Carthusians
in the work of translation:*

Mr Robin Bruce Lockhart

Sr Maureen Scrine

Miss Carmel Brett

Sr Jane Margaret Cliston, VHM

Fr Richard Catterall

Fr Gordon Mursell

Mr Leo McDonnell

Mme Pamela de Villaine

*Thanks are also owed to Mrs Margaret Holleran for her help
in typing the manuscript*

Contents

Note: The bracketed numbers appearing in the body of the text refer to the Statutes of the Carthusian Order, the first number indicating the book, the second the chapter, and the third the paragraph. If only two numbers are given, the first is the chapter, the second the paragraph.

Preface

Books on the Carthusian life are already available. Why another? Because there is no book in which Carthusians themselves, and in particular, contemporary ones, speak to other Carthusians of the intimate details, the unexpected crises, the everyday challenges of their existence in the desert, thus lifting the veil beyond the pious spiritual theology that has so long been provided for the casual onlooker.

This book is therefore destined for those who thirst to have a look at 'things as they are' in the Charterhouse. Apart from 'The Poor Communities', written in 1993, all of the present selections were written in the decade from 1975 to 1985, and spring from the pen either of a Prior of the Order, normally speaking to his community in the chapter sermons prescribed for some dozen occasions throughout the year, or from that of a Novice Master, addressing his novitiate in the weekly conferences. In this account, therefore, although explanatory notes will be provided when necessary, a basic familiarity with the structure of Carthusian life is presumed (e.g. that there is a Midnight Office, which is one of only three daily gatherings for liturgical prayer in common; that the Fathers live their solitary life in modest and austere hermitages around a cloister, while the Brothers live theirs fulfilling daily chores around the monastery, etc.) Here, we gaze past the horizons of structure to the Mystery that both sustains and outstrips it.

One aspect of this Mystery of particular contemporary interest, we believe, can be envisaged as a paradox, although clearly conformed to traditional spirituality: to seek the Absolute, and him alone, we must relinquish it, since it so swiftly shows itself to be an abstraction or and idol (cf. chapter

3); humble, fraternal love is finally seen, not as an obstacle, but as the very condition, of authentic solitude (chapter 5). Yet, such a happy 'harmony of opposites', with its salutary effects on both the spiritual and the psychological levels, should hardly surprise us if the aim of our pursuit is to regain that harmony and wholeness in God which was the lot of our race on the first morning of creation, and which is also the challenge and promise of the New Creation in Christ. Hence, slowly, through the course of the years in the Charterhouse, the corporal and spiritual components of our being and our prayer are seamlessly integrated (chapter 11); the personal interior dimension is joined to the communitarian and liturgical (chapter 4). Indeed, purity of heart, the goal of monks throughout the ages, can be defined as that simplicity which receives all, even and only God himself, at every moment, through all the channels of our faculties, in daily events, in all of creation (chapters 8, 24, 25). *Hesychia* is but the breathing of the Holy Spirit, a stability in the Spirit of the risen Christ (chapter 22) that is attained only at the price of our entirely letting go: of allowing our complications, our resistances, and our narrow, twisted *a priori* to be burned away under the desert sun (chapter 18); at the price of our willingness to slaughter 'Isaac', so that he who truly 'laughs' with the serenity of God's Joy may be born again from the ashes of holocaust (chapter 15). The Carthusian knows that this hidden gestation takes a lifetime, and that is why he is silent. The birth pangs are severe (more severe than he ever expected); but the cry of birth is a shout of victory that opens upon eternity.

Prologue

A Joy Unknown to the World

OUR FATHER ST BRUNO TO HIS CARTHUSIAN SONS*

To my brothers whom I love in Christ above everything else, greetings from your brother, Bruno.

Now that I have heard from our dear brother Landuin a detailed and moving account of how firm you are in your resolve to follow a path of life so commendable and in accord with right reason, and have learned of your ardent love and unflagging zeal for all that pertains to moral rectitude and the fullness of Christian maturity, my spirit rejoices in the Lord. I truly exalt, and am swept away by my impulse to praise and thanksgiving; yet, at the same time, I bitterly lament. I rejoice, as is only right, over the ripening fruit of your virtues; but I blush, and bemoan my own condition, since I wallow so listless and inactive in the filth of my sins.

Rejoice, therefore, my beloved brothers, over the lot of overflowing happiness that has fallen to you, and for the grace of God that you have received in such abundance. Rejoice that you have succeeded in escaping the countless dangers and shipwrecks of this storm-tossed world, and have reached a quiet corner in the security of a hidden harbour. Many would like to join you, and many there are also who make a considerable effort to do so, but fail in their attempt. What is more, many are shut out even after having attained it, since it was not in the plan of God to give them this grace.

Therefore, my brothers, count it a certitude, proven time and time again: whoever has experienced such an enviable good, and

---

*The only writings indisputably from the pen of St Bruno that have come down to us are the following two letters, written from Calabria during the last ten years of his life.

subsequently lost it for whatever reasons, will grieve over his loss to the end of his days, if he has any regard or concern for the salvation of his soul.

As regards you lay monks, brothers, so close to my heart, I have only this to say: my soul glorifies the Lord, since I can perceive the glories of his mercy toward you from the account of your beloved father and prior, who boasts a great deal about you, and rejoices over you. I share in this joy, since God in his power never ceases to inscribe on your hearts, however little education you may have, not only love, but understanding. That is to say, when you are careful and zealous to observe a genuine obedience, conceived not only as the carrying out of God's commands, but as the original key to the spiritual life and its final stamp of authenticity, demanding as it does deep humility and outstanding patience, as well as sincere love for the Lord and our brothers, then it is clear that you are gathering with relish no less than the most delectable and life-giving fruits of Holy Scripture.

So, my brothers, abide in that which you have attained, and avoid like the plague that baneful crowd of would-be monks who in reality are as empty as can be, peddling their writings, and speaking in hushed tones about things they neither cherish nor understand, but rather contradict by their words and actions. They are lazy, and wander from place to place, slandering all those who are conscientious and dedicated, and imagining themselves worthy of praise if they blacken the name of those who really are. To them, anything resembling discipline or obedience is loathsome.

As for our brother Landuin, I had intended to keep him here on account of his rather serious and recurrent illnesses; but he would have none of it, claiming that there could be nothing worthwhile for him, no health or joy nor zest for life, apart from you. With repeated sighs, and a veritable gushing fountain of tears for you, he laid before me how much you mean to him, and the unadulterated affection he bears for you in the Lord. As a result, I have not wanted to force the issue, lest I cause grief either to him or to you, who are so dear to me for your maturity and excellence of spirit. Wherefore, my brothers, I am very serious in my request, at once humble and insistent, that you manifest by your deeds the love you bear in your heart for your prior and beloved father by kindly and attentively providing him with everything he needs for the various requirements of his health. He may be unwilling to go along with what your loving solicitude may dictate, preferring to jeopardize his life and health rather than be found lacking in some point of external observance. After all, this is normally inadmissible, and he might blush to hold the first rank among you, and yet trail in these matters, fearing that you might become negligent or lukewarm on his account. Yet, I hardly think there is any danger of that; so, I hereby grant you the necessary authority to take my place in this particular, and respectfully compel him to accept whatever you accord him for his health.

As for me, brothers, I would have you know that the only desire I have, after God, is to come and see you. As soon as I can, God willing, I will do just that.

Farewell.

ST BRUNO'S LETTER TO RAOUL LE VERD

To my esteemed friend Raoul, Dean of the Cathedral Chapter at Rheims, I, Bruno, send my greeting, as all my heartfelt affection toward you bids me.

The loyalty you have shown during our long and mellowed friendship is all the more beautiful and remarkable in that it is only rarely found. For, even though a great distance and many years lie between us, your kindly sentiments have always been with me. This is certainly clear enough from your wonderful letters, in which you have professed your friendship over and over again, and from the many other indications you have given of it, including the favours you have so generously shown, both to me, and to Brother Bernard on my account. For all this, I give you my thanks, dear friend, not in a way which could ever be commensurate with what you deserve of me, but springing, at least, from the deepest source of sincere love.

I sent a messenger with a letter to you some time ago, one who had proved reliable on other occasions; but since he has not yet returned, I thought it best to send you one of the brethren. He can give you a fuller account of how things are here by word of mouth than I could ever do with pen and ink.

I assure you, first of all, that my health is good, thinking that the news will not be unwelcome to you. I wish that I could say the same

*for my soul! The external situation is as satisfactory as could be
desired; but I stand as a beggar before the mercy of God, praying
that he will heal all the infirmities of my soul, and fulfil all my
desires with his bounty.*

*I am living in the wilderness of Calbria, far removed from habi-
tation. There are some brethren with me, some of whom are very
well educated, and they are keeping assiduous watch for their Lord,
so as to open to him at once when he knocks. I could never even
begin to tell you how charming and pleasant it is. The temperatures
are mild, the air is healthful; a broad plain, delightful to behold,
stretches between the mountains along their entire length, bursting
with fragrant meadows and flowery fields. One could hardly describe
the impression made by the gently rolling hills on all sides, with
their cool and shady glens tucked away, and such an abundance of
refreshing springs, brooks and streams. Besides all this, there are
verdant gardens, and all sorts of fruit-bearing trees.*

*Yet why dwell on such things as these? The man of true insight
has other delights, far more useful and attractive, because divine. It
is true, though, that our rather feeble nature is renewed and finds
new life in such perspectives, wearied by its spiritual pursuits and
austere mode of life. It is like a bow, which soon wears out and runs
the risk of becoming useless, if it is kept continually taut.*

*In any case, what benefits and divine exultation the silence and
solitude of the desert hold in store for those who love it, only those
who have experienced it can know. For here men of strong will can
enter into themselves and remain there as much as they like, diligently
cultivating the seeds of virtue, and eating the fruits of Paradise with
joy. Here, they can acquire the eye that wounds the Bridegroom
with love by the limpidity of its gaze, and whose purity allows them
to see God himself. Here they can observe a busy leisure, and rest
in quiet activity. Here also, God crowns his athletes for their stern
struggle with the hoped-for reward: a peace unknown to the world,
and joy in the Holy Spirit.*

*Such a way of life is exemplified by Rachel, who was preferred by
Jacob for her beauty even though she bore fewer children than Leah,
with her less penetrating eyes. Contemplation, to be sure, has fewer
offspring than does action, and yet Joseph and Benjamin were the
favourites of their father. This life is the best part chosen by Mary,
never to be taken away from her. It is also that extraordinarily*

beautiful Shunammite, the only one in Israel able to take care of David and keep him warm in his old age. I could only wish, brother, that you, too, had such an exclusive love for her, so that, lost in her embrace, you burned with divine love! If only a love like this would take possession of you! Immediately, all the glory in the world would seem like so much dirt to you, whatever the smooth words and false attractions she offered to deceive you. Wealth, and its concomitant anxieties, you would cast off without a thought as a burden to the freedom of the spirit. You would want no more of pleasure either, harmful as it is to both body and soul.

You know very well who it is that says to us, 'He who loves the world, and the things in the world, such as the lust of the flesh, the lust of the eyes, and ambition, does not have the love of the Father abiding in him'; also 'Friendship with the world is enmity with God'. What could be so evil and destructive, then, so unfortunate, or so much the mark of a crazed and headstrong spirit, as to put yourself at odds with the one whose power you cannot resist, and whose righteous vengeance you could never hope to escape? Surely we are not stronger than he! Surely you do not think he will leave unpunished in the end all the affronts and contempt he receives, merely because his patient solicitude now incites us to repentance! For what could be more perverted, more reckless and contrary to nature and right order, than to love the creature more than the Creator, what passes away more than what lasts forever, or to seek rather the goods of earth than those of heaven?

So, what do you think ought to be done, dear friend? What else, but to trust in the exhortation of God himself, and to believe in the Truth which cannot deceive? For he calls out to everyone, saying, 'Come to me, all who labour and are heavy laden, and I will give you rest.' Is it not, after all, a most ridiculous and fruitless labour to be swollen with lust, continually to be tortured with anxiety and worry, fear and sorrow, for the objects of your passion? Is there any heavier burden than to have one's spirit thus cast down into the abyss from the sublime peak of its natural dignity – the veritable quintessence of right order gone awry? Flee, my brother, from these unending miseries and disturbances; leave the raging storms of this world for the secure and quiet harbour of the port.

For you know very well what Wisdom in person has to say to us: 'Whoever does not renounce all that he has, cannot be my disciple.'

Who cannot perceive what a beautiful thing it is, how beneficial, and how delightful besides, to remain in the school of Christ under the guidance of the Holy Spirit, there to learn that divine philosophy which alone shows the way to true happiness?

So, you must consider the facts very honestly: if the love of God does not succeed in attracting you, nor considerations of self-interest spur you on in the face of such enormous rewards, at least dire necessity and the fear of chastisement ought to compel you to move in this direction. For you know the promise that binds you, and to whom it was made. It is none other than the omnipotent and awesome One to whom you consecrated yourself as a pleasing and wholly acceptable offering. To him it is not permissible to lie, nor would it do any good, besides; for he does not let himself be mocked with impunity.

You remember, after all, the time you and I, and Fulk One-eye, were together in the little garden adjoining Adam's house, where I was staying at the time. We had been discussing for some while, as I recall, the false attractions and ephemeral riches of this present life, and comparing them with the joys of eternal glory. As a result, we were inflamed with divine love, and we promised, determined and vowed to abandon the fleeting shadows of this world at the earliest opportunity, and lay hold of the eternal by taking a monastic habit. We would, indeed, have done so forthwith; but Fulk went off to Rome, and we postponed our resolution in the expectation of his return. He was delayed, however, and other things got in the way as well, so that, in the end, fervour vanished, and resolve grew cold.

So, what is left, dear friend, but to absolve yourself as quickly as possible from the obligations of such a debt? Otherwise, you run the risk of incurring the wrath of the All-powerful for such serious and long-standing deception, not to mention the frightful torments that are its consequence. What potentate, after all, of this world would ever leave himself unavenged if he were cheated by any of his subjects of a promised gift, especially if he considered it to be of outstanding value? So, never mind me, simply listen to the psalmist, or rather to the Holy Spirit, who declares: 'Make your vows to the Lord your God, and perform them; let all around him bring gifts to him who is to be feared, who cuts off the spirit of princes, who is terrible to the kings of the earth.' It is the voice of the Lord you hear, the voice of your God, the one who is feared, who cuts off the spirit of princes, who is terrible to the kings of the earth! For what reason does the Spirit of God make such a point of this, if not to prod you into acquitting yourself of your vow? Why do you find it burdensome, since it entails no sacrifice or reduction of your goods, and heaps up benefits rather for yourself than for the one who receives what you pay?

Do not let the deceptive lure of riches hold you back, since they cannot remedy the real poverty of our soul; nor let your position detain you, since you cannot occupy it without notable jeopardy to the spiritual life. For, it would be repugnant and wicked indeed, if I may say so, to convert to your own use the goods of another, since you are, in fact, their steward, and not their proprietor. In addition, if you should become desirous of vaunting your wealth in empty show, and keep a large retinue for this purpose, will it not be necessary, in some way, to snatch from one person what you bestow with great largesse on someone else? Your own resources, after all, would not suffice. Yet such a procedure would be neither generous nor to good effect, for nothing can be considered generous which is not at the same time just.

You must also be careful not to be allured away from the exigencies of divine love in your attention to the needs of the archbishop. He has great confidence in your counsel and relies heavily upon it; but it is not always an easy matter to give advice that is both useful and just. It is rather divine love which proves itself the more useful, precisely to the extent that it is more in accord with right reason. For what could be beneficial and right, so fitting, and connatural to human nature, as to love the Good? Yet what other good can compare with God? Indeed, what other good is there besides God? Whence it comes that the soul that has attained some degree of holiness, and has experienced in some small measure the incomparable loveliness, beauty, and splendour of this Good, is set on fire with love, and cries out: 'My soul is thirsting for God, the God of my life; when shall I enter and see the face of God?'

My sincere hope, brother, is that you will not spurn the counsel of a friend, nor turn a deaf ear to the words the Holy Spirit speaks (within). As my very close friend, I hope you will grant these desires of mine, and put an end to my long vigil in your regard. Otherwise, I will continue to be tortured with solicitude, anxiety and fear for you. God forbid that you should die before acquitting yourself of your vow; for, in that case, you would leave me pining away with unremitting sorrow, without ever any hope of consolation.

My request, therefore, is that you will agree to go on pilgrimage to St Nicholas, and from there make your way to us. Thus, you will be able to see the one who loves you as no one else, and we will be able to speak face to face about our religious life, and how things are going, and whatever else might be a matter of common interest. I trust in the Lord that you will not regret any trouble involved in such a journey.

This letter is not as succinct as it ordinarily ought to be; but that is only because I do not have the joy of your presence. As a result, I desired to prolong our conversation, at least in writing, and thus have the pleasure of your company.

So, brother, stay in good health. Accept my ardent wish that you will take my words very much to heart.

Bruno

P.S. Would you send us the Life *of St Remigius? It is impossible to obtain it here.*

Farewell.

Introductory

1

Inventing of the Order 1084

St Bruno, Pathway to Life*

We are asked to turn towards our Blessed Father not so much because we can see in him a perfect example of one or more particular virtues but because he shows us the path to follow to attain the peerless grace of our vocation: a grace, as we are told in the Carta,† acquired thanks to the intercession of the Blessed Virgin Mary.

In this respect, Bruno fulfils the very humble yet irreplaceable role of the man from whom we receive that infusion of divine grace whereby we can listen in solitude to the unique Good and in which we should be thirsting for the presence of the living God. This very day, Bruno is our pathway to life, because he is, in the risen Christ, alive and with us his children. But he is also this source of the divine because he was the *first* to receive the call of the Holy Spirit, placing himself under the tutelage of Divine Wisdom here in these mountains where we live today.

One has only to have been to the site of St Bruno's chapel in mid-winter, when it is covered with a thick mantle of snow, to be aware that the supernatural fruitfulness of our Blessed Father is not the outcome of sublime thoughts of a speculative nature but of the very real and arduous life which led the first Carthusian hermits to silence of heart through the shedding of earthly ties, a life of complete simplicity.

---

*Sermon given by Father General at the General Chapter of 1983, in view of the celebration of the ninth centenary of the founding of the Order in 1084.
†Official document of the Chapter.

Our Father Saint Bruno: this title does not raise thoughts in our minds of lengthy doctrine nor of elaborate teaching but rather the existence of a mature master who allowed himself to be seduced by the goodness of God and gave everything up for its sake. He has little else to tell us except his life in the desert where, in silent vigil, the pure gaze of love wounds the beloved's heart.

Let us return now to the affirmation of the Carta: all the good that comes to us in our life is due to the ministry of Bruno. Naturally for us he is a unique example to follow; but that is not his principal role, which is rather to draw from God himself, through the intercession of Mary, that longing to meet the Most High, the All-Beautiful, and to imbue us with this longing unceasingly, so that it takes possession of our heart and drives us inexorably towards the encounter with the face of God.

To be a Carthusian is to receive from Bruno that stirring from the Holy Spirit which likens us to Christ in his paschal mystery as he is drawn towards the Father. At the opening of this chapter we were strongly recommended to renew our sense of God: a call applicable to all mankind but how much more so to the heirs of Bruno! Sometimes it is impossible not to be seized by a feeling of dizziness when one thinks of the warning in the Statues:* the higher the road we travel, the more we risk being weighed down by human nature, sliding back and finding ourselves much lower than when we started.

Left to ourselves we would never be able to avoid such an inevitable degeneration. To live in God's presence in silence and solitude is a grace flowing from the heart of God into that of St Bruno and from his into our own. The daily reminder of our limitations, when faced with the harsh contours of our vocation, never ceases to remind us of the need to rely on the channel which is St Bruno.

---

*The Statutes of the Carthusian Order are based on the Customs of Guigo, fifth Prior of the Grande Chartreuse, written in 1127. They were revised and augmented a number of times throughout the centuries. Most recently, they underwent a massive updating after the Second Vatican Council (1971), and some minor retouching after the promulgation of the New Code of Canon Law (1987).

From the remarkable gentleness revealed in his letters, when he opens his heart to those he loves, we sense that in the end this vocation, when in touch with its deepest source, is not an exploit achieved through force or violence, but the fruit of a calm confidence in the one who gave himself to us once and for all. Confirmation of the authenticity of our dependence on St Bruno, it seems to me, lies precisely in the quality of the love which binds us to our brothers in both confidence and peace.

We are told by the Carta that God has made us one family through a share in the unity of the Divine Persons, through the mediation of St Bruno. Almost by his very essence he has become, so to speak, a leaven binding us one to another. Let us stress, once again, that it is his person and not just his discreet counsel that fulfils this role. Because this man of profound heart committed himself totally to a life face to face with God in what would appear to be an exclusive relationship with him, he is forever abounding in a gentleness which flows down on us and establishes us, in turn, in the unity of that Carthusian family which has become the transparent milieu in which we can hope to contemplate God.

Master Bruno, enamoured of the Unique and free from all that is transient, man of serenity and joy, you who so longed to rejoin your far-distant brothers in the desert of Chartreuse, at the start of this year which we wish to devote to letting ourselves be transformed by you, look upon this little Carthusian family whose unity we at the General Chapter symbolize by the very diversity of our backgrounds. Look at the same time on the living God, before whom you stand and by whom you have been assigned the task of imbuing us with an ever more ardent love of him.

We offer ourselves to the light of which you are the messenger, and we praise the Lord by whom you have been given to us as Father, thanks to the intercession of Mary ever Virgin. Amen.

I

Solitude and Fraternal Love

Chap 6 MT. Go in Room and Shut the Door.

" Prayer is nothing but Love "
We only go into Solitude for Jesus Christ.

2

The Degrees of Solitude

The one thing that improves society is solitude

Prayer and solitude are intimately related. Our view of solitude, therefore, and the way we live it, will have an effect on the quality of our prayer. In fact, there are many different attitudes possible toward solitude, which correspond to extremely diverse levels of openness in mind and heart. The psychological deformations of solitude that leave us prisoners of our egoism are numerous, and constitute one of the subtlest obstacles of the authenticity of our prayer. Entry into the genuine solitude to which God calls us can only be the result of a series of conquests that often demand nothing less than a veritable reformation of our interior life.

Simplicity not costing only everything (T. S. Eliot)
Jesus teaches us to die to ourselves graciously.

SOLITUDE BASED ON OBEDIENCE

The Statutes contain some very strict rules on solitude for us to follow. To be a good solitary, therefore, is it sufficient to be faithful to these prescriptions, or, if circumstances oblige us otherwise, to seek permission of the Superior?

Reading the Statutes in this way obviously corresponds to a real spiritual need; we are not pure spirits, free from all material constraint; our fidelity to the inner call of the Spirit must have the support of a framework and be formed and guided by a permanent structure. Seen in this way, solitude is the object of a sort of gradual appropriation: to enable us to enter truly into solitude, it is very helpful for us to be provided with a clearly articulated framework.

The characteristic grace of this approach to solitude is obedience. All the spiritual ardour that is expressed by our separation

from the world and silence with our brothers is marshalled
under the standard of obedience. In this case, solitude is one
observance among many, which derive their worth solely from
'the blessing of obedience' (7.8).

The most primitive episodes in the history of Israel are an
illustration of such dispositions before God. Abraham, for
example, leaves his family when God so commands him and
journeys to the land of Canaan where he remains ever a stranger
and a pilgrim. Obedience plunges him into a solitude that is
frequently austere, but which he gladly accepts as a pledge of
heavenly promises.

Still more illuminating is the example of Israel in the desert.
Despite their dullness and apathy, the children of the promise
paid heed to Moses and set out for the desert of Sinai. For
forty years, obedience kept them marching through the desert
toward a promised land whose blessings remained elusive.
Indeed, it was only through a very strict submission, demanded,
to be sure, by the love of God, but taking the form of often
severe interventions, that this epic of Israel unfolded. It was the
crucible in which the People of God was forged, a saga whose
climax was the revelation of the Lord on Sinai. This first exodus
remains forever the mysterious sign of the second exodus which
the Son of God himself was to accomplish, drawing us up into
his own passage from this world to the Father.

Solitude, considered as one observance among others as a
point of the rule, gives in the end a rich but incomplete idea
of what God is expecting from us. We should beware of scorning
it, since it is a harbinger of grace and has its role to play in the
life of each one of us. Nonetheless, we cannot be content with
it: it must be subsumed into an attitude that is wider and
deeper, wherein solitude is no longer something imposed from
without, but rather flows from an inner necessity.

SOLITUDE AS SEPARATION FROM OTHERS

Entry into solitude inexorably implies a decision to separate
ourselves, to cut ourselves off from those around us. Here,
again, the Statutes provide memories, vistas which show that

this way of viewing solitude is well founded. 'Love for our brothers should show itself firstly in respect for their solitude' (4.4). We avoid all unnecessary contacts; we are invited to discourage friends who would like to see us; we categorically refuse any apostolate that would compromise the simplicity of our silence. One could draw up in this way an entire catalogue of prohibitions that we wholeheartedly embrace, in the knowledge that, however painful they may be both for ourselves and for others, they are an indispensable condition of authentic solitude. This array of safeguards for avoiding contact with our neighbour, in their deepest significance, could be termed spiritual virginity.

It is easy to perceive in such an attitude a reproduction of the frame of mind that prevailed for centuries among the people of Israel in the Promised Land, which gradually affirmed their identity against their enemies and powerful neighbours. There was a veritable intransigence in their refusal to mingle, particularly at the level of the spiritual élite. It was an absolutely crucial point, a matter of life and death. Before their entry into the Promised Land, the Lord himself had vigorously enjoined them to avoid all compromise with the cultures they would meet. If they really wanted to become God's people, they would have to break with the pagans that surrounded them, and this refusal to communicate was the very guarantee of their own existence. The people knew that countless tendencies to betrayal lurked within them and this made the friends of God all the more adamant in their efforts to cut the nation off from whatever might contaminate it. This was an indispensable step on the way toward a loftier understanding of the nation's vocation.

Hence, it would be wrong for us to condemn such an attitude on the pretext that it is too negative. It may be true that this approach is incomplete and incapable of leading us all the way to our destination; nonetheless, solitude, in order to be itself, must always retain this flavour of courageous refusal to compromise. The history of monasticism demonstrates that only those religious families that were adamant in insisting on this rule retained their solitary character; all the others, doubtless because their vocation lay elsewhere, swiftly adopted a cenobitic lifestyle, and, in most cases, resumed habitual contact with the world.

Nonetheless, solitude as refusal is incapable of producing peace and balance within; in a way, it rather corresponds to an inner amputation, to a spiritual and affective mutilation. It is normal that it should end up giving rise to anxiety and nervous tension, since it encourages the person in an artificial attitude. Doubtless, it already qualifies as a form of love for God, but it sometimes dispenses with love for our brothers. In fact, the external separation that we impose on ourselves is only legitimate in the measure that it is assumed by a higher and more open form of solitude.

SOLITUDE CLOSED IN ON ITSELF

The negative attitude about which we have been speaking is a first and perhaps infantile reaction to the discovery of solitude: we are all caught up in the joy of giving ourselves over to it entirely, even at the price of painful sacrifices. Nevertheless, a more positive attitude normally follows. We make ourselves at home, so to speak, in our solitude; by a sort of instinctive reaction, we tend to organize it as a little self-sufficient world apart, with its own laws and its proper spirit. Gradually, we become aware of the advantages and value of this life in solitude and, naturally enough, we find a certain security there. The temptation then will be to judge the rest of the world as functioning for the benefit of this solitude, which seems purer and more fertile in spiritual values. The solitary will be led to consider his desert as the centre of the world. He has found life there himself and he knows that the rest of humanity has need of this life. Hence, he opens out to others, but only to take them and reduce them to his own dimensions. His solitude remains closed.

This situation is strongly reminiscent of the Old Law, against which St Paul so vigorously warned the first Christians, prey to the lure of a well-defined security that would result from the fulfilment of ritual. The Old Covenant was instituted by the Lord as a sort of pedagogy that would progressively lead

Israel to an authentic interior openness to the Spirit. Only the 'remnant' followed this path, while the rest turned the Law into a hard and unyielding shell that no longer prepared the way of the Lord.

It would be unjust to condemn out of hand a solitude that is conceived as a world unto itself, destined to conduct one to his or her deepest centre. Nonetheless, it cannot be denied that a too exclusive view of the desert leads almost of necessity to an attitude of instinctive superiority, a sort of caste pride. One is tempted to live as though solitude were an end in itself rather than being simply a transparency to God.

THE SEDUCTION OF THE FAR EAST

This is a particular form of solitude closed in on itself which today attracts those in pursuit of contemplation. The age-old techniques of the Far East, hidden for centuries, are now enjoying considerable publicity, with their promise of recollection, self-discovery and the incomparable joys of the deepest interior silence. There is no doubt that these techniques, in their most authentic and conscientious manifestations, allow those who apply themselves wholeheartedly to reach an inner balance and peace that exert an undeniable appeal. The illumination afforded is genuinely contemplative.

What we encounter here is a radical mobilization of the virtualities of the soul created in the image and likeness of God. To the extent that one can, through natural techniques, force oneself from interior division and gaze upon the soul as the incomparable mirror of the Divinity, one enters into the domain of an authentic contemplation. After the necessary purifications, the soul considers itself in its union with the created universe, a still more admirable image of the Creator. How could we resist being lured by such prospects, if nothing more marvellous were offered us?

Nevertheless, a discordant note is struck in this optimistic view by the tragedy of Job. He also had found his balance and his happiness in sincerely accomplishing all that was required of him to free himself from evil; but, without realizing it, he had reduced God to his own dimensions, and in his naïveté, never even imagined that there could be other ways of being faithful to his inner inclinations. His distress knows no bounds when everything collapses under the onslaught of a Stranger who penetrates his closed system and bursts it wide open. He is in the process of discovering God, a God who is not his own size but, on the contrary, totally other, and who, precisely in this complete otherness, is his only true source of happiness.

In the end, that is how it is with all solitudes closed in on themselves, whether it be those of the Old Covenant, or those of the Eastern techniques: they entail no real gift of oneself; rather, they put the rubber stamp on the created world as sufficient in and to itself. There is indeed an image of the transcendent God, but it is no more than an image. The day the prototype (uncreated model) arrives to shatter this security, 'the mountains melt at his presence' (Isaiah 63:19).

THE SOLITUDE OF GOD'S OWN HEART

True solitude, really worthy of the name, must trace its way back to its source. It is not obedience to an external law, nor a flight from others, nor a world closed on itself, but an encounter with the living God. Solitude is a gratuitous gift, destined to be received in all humility; it is not our own creation, nor that of anyone else. It does not consist in doing anything, nor in trying to become somebody: it is a sharing in the solitude of God. This divine solitude is not, as is sometimes said rather too glibly, his isolation with respect to creatures so different from him: it is rather the fullness that he finds in the intimacy with his Word, springing from his bosom, and returning to him in the Spirit. It is in and through Jesus Christ that we will penetrate into the true solitude which is God.

3

Beyond the Absolute

To become a Carthusian, the desire alone does not suffice. It is not enough to be warmly welcomed into the community and to receive all the elements of a good formation. He alone remains in the Charterhouse who has felt a call in the very centre of his soul which is more powerful than any of the contradictory forces within and around him. The Carthusian vocation is a work of God. Our human co-operation is perhaps more indispensable than in any other context, but we are well aware that we are utterly incapable of bringing the work to fruition left to our own devices.

First of all, then, there is a call. Though purely interior, it seeks to realize itself within an exterior, institutional framework whose rigidity may seem surprising. Once the decision has been made, the discovery of Carthusian life in practice opens up a world in which the paradoxes are often difficult to accept. The stages of the discovery are often as follows.

THE SEDUCTION OF THE ABSOLUTE

He alone who has experienced this seduction can understand. When God calls, it is so self-evident that all words and arguments are left behind. When God reveals himself, there is no room for discussion; it is he alone whom we meet, even if we can find no way of explaining this to others. For want of a better term, let us speak here of 'the Absolute'. Such a way of speaking has its disadvantages, as must any discourse about God; yet, it brings to the fore what is the distinctive attribute of an in-depth revelation of God: it is he and no one else.

We recognize him immediately even if we have never met him
before. There is nothing with which we can compare him. He
reveals himself truly as perfection itself and takes hold of our
hearts at once. A thirst is born within us which nothing can
quench except the Absolute. Anyone who has received this
wound sets out in quest of the means of reaching the Absolute
in so far as it is possible in this life. No doubt the means
available will always be inadequate, but we long to do all that
is in our power to attain it.

To give oneself to God for his sake

To the one who sets out on this quest, the Charterhouse appears
from the outset as a world he already knew, sight unseen. It
seems to hold the answers, as if by instinct, to his search.
There seems to be a sort of connivance between what one is
told and what one would have said oneself. To give oneself to
God for his sake. To live for him alone. To renounce everything
that is not God and find in him the fulfilment of all we seek.
Not only do we find these formulas written down, but we have
the feeling that they are actually being lived, even if we realize
that the framework is in many ways rather shabby and apparently a bit shrivelled up.

A complete break with the world

A Charterhouse couples in a quite inseparable manner both
the heady prescriptions for union with God and a brutal rupture
from what in traditional monastic language is called 'the world'.
Despite certain misrepresentations, there is nothing in this of
Manichaeism, pessimism or contempt for those who are part
of 'the world'. The world is the whole of humanity engaged in
the splendid enterprise of co-operating with the action of the
Creator. It is man tending towards God across the whole spec-
trum of his creation. It is religious man who reflects the face
of God in Christ through a thousand forms of apostolate.
All of this is good and all reflects God; but none of it *is* God.
Choosing God consequently implies a separation from everything that is not God without even considering all that is
involved, and we would not dream of compromising on its

exigencies. Even the most wonderful of his creations is nothing compared with him and he it is whom we seek.

Turning unreservedly to God

We have referred to the seduction of the Absolute. The expression is not too strong. It brings to mind the words of Jeremiah: 'You have seduced me, Lord, and I let myself be seduced'. In the joy of finding God, all decisions become easy, however much we may still be obliged to reach them only after careful consideration. One realizes that there can be no other solution; a great threshold must now be crossed which commits us totally and exclusively to the search for God. We must cast ourselves into the abyss, believe in the Absolute, and cut ourselves off from all that is not God.

To be resurrected with Christ

Only Jesus, through his death and resurrection, was able to fulfil this dream completely; to respond with his whole being to the call of God, to cast himself onto him and to find himself again fully in his embrace. To choose the Carthusian way is therefore to immerse oneself in a particularly expressive and effective way in the Resurrection of the Saviour. There must be a death, of which we are not always fully conscious at the start, but which gradually extends its effects into all the dimensions of our lives. Yet there is also a birth into a new life which truly brings us into intimacy with God.

THE PATHS OF THE ABSOLUTE

Once settled in a Charterhouse, we soon learn that the radical choice to live for God alone must necessarily implant itself on our entire concrete existence, our perceptions and our social interactions, however fragile and unstable they may be. We begin to learn what this entails and how difficult it is. We cannot go into detail here, but let it suffice to point out how this choice, apparently so purely spiritual, has to express itself in all its radicality within the limits of time and space in which a Carthusian lives out his life.

The 'limits' of a Charterhouse

Historians who study the foundation of Charterhouses in the
Middle Ages usually discover something which shocks them if
they are unfamiliar with Carthusian life. They find that Carthusians, once decided on a foundation and a site for it, began by
setting up 'limits' around the site which effectively define the
boundary between themselves and the world. It did not matter
whether or not the surrounding land already belonged to the
Carthusians; for, if not, the objective was to acquire it or to
obtain privileges which would ensure that no other human
habitation should exist within its boundaries. This was considered by the early Carthusians to be an essential condition
for a foundation. The monastery had to be the heart of an area
of genuine solitude. The division between the Charterhouse
and the world needed to be clearly defined. Once this had been
achieved, a further set of limits was laid down which detailed
the boundaries which the monks were not to cross if they
wished to be faithful to the spirit of solitude. The novice who
makes profession knows that he is committing himself to remain
within these boundaries, which constitute his desert, his
solitude.

It would be shabby to see in this some kind of acquisitive
instinct or power-seeking on the part of Carthusians. Even if
the question of boundaries has frequently involved them in
lawsuits or disputes with their neighbours, one has to understand this fierce determination to cut themselves off from the
world as giving rather bald expression to their feeling of really
having chosen God and nothing but God. The Absolute has
burned itself into their lives in a frighteningly demanding way.
To tumble definitively into God, as we have said, is to enclose
oneself within him both spiritually and physically. The 'limits'
of a Charterhouse are the material sign that we have enclosed
ourselves within God. 'Your life is hidden with Christ in God,'
said St Paul. Such is the goal of the Carthusian: to be hidden,
to compel others to respect his anonymity, to be forgotten. Yet,
it is also to impose on himself the restriction of no longer being
able to wander about, nor to go here and there as his fancy
might lead him. He is anchored in God, even in body, even in

the basic human freedom which has the entire earth, bestowed by the Creator, at its disposal.

The meaning of the vows

It is obvious that religious vows are not a monopoly of the Carthusians. Yet, perhaps we are approaching a time when only the Carthusians will still have a lifestyle that corresponds to the frame of mind that prevailed in the monastic circles in which the vows were born fifteen hundred years ago. The vows, in their deepest reality, are strictly modelled on the structures of Carthusian life.

The origins of the first monastic vows are obscure. Nevertheless, it would seem that they came into being spontaneously, in order to deal with instability among monks, whether as regards the vocation itself, or as regards their tendency to wander from one monastery to another. The vows were a sort of 'limit', in the sense discussed in the previous paragraph. They mark a complete break in the life of the monk, in that he sees himself obliged to remain fixed in God, through a decision freely made when he enters the monastery, and binds himself to it in profession. Without wishing to deny the juridical exaggerations which have grown up around the vows, we must know how to rediscover the deep inspiration underlying them. Their authors probably did not realize it clearly, but they were following a very real inspiration.

The intention of one taking monastic vows is to make a truly absolute gift of himself or herself to God. The seduction of the Absolute implies the desire to imprint within ourselves a reminder of the Absolute which prepares us to meet it. That choice, which made us give up everything for him, is one that we wish to see mould our whole interior being. We must therefore make a complete break with the outside world: the vow of stability corresponding in each one of us to the concrete existence of limits. Above all, it is important to draw a clear line between the flight from God, to which all the weight of our fallen nature disposes us, and the choice of a love ever faithful to God: the vow of obedience.

To the superficial observer, the monk thus finds himself enmeshed in a network of obligations that bind and paralyse

him, and, in fact, that is sometimes the way his life is described.
The reality, though, is exactly the opposite. The vows are the
unbreachable line of demarcation between the realm of
Absolute, the zone in which we wish God to be undisputed
ruler, and everything else. They are the gateway to divine
freedom.

Comparisons

In order to have a better understanding of the radical break
imprinted on a monk's life by Carthusian solitude, it might be
helpful to view it alongside other forms of solitary life.

THE HERMIT. The hermit is certainly a man of solitude, but by
the very nature of things, as history bears ample witness, also
a man liable to evolve in many different ways. He may end up
as the founder of a cenobitic abbey, or as a preacher, or be
summoned to the episcopate as a pastor of souls. He, too, has
therefore felt the burning desire of the Absolute, but has not
perceived the call to bury himself in it once and for all. His
solitude could indeed last all his life; but it could also very well
be only a staging post on the road towards another vocation to
which the Lord is calling him.

THE CAMALDOLESE. Son of St Benedict, he places his solitude in
a context not unlike that of the hermit. It is but one among
many forms of worshipping God. Remember, for instance, that
the apostles of Poland were the first Camaldolese. There is
nothing wrong with having teacher and preachers, etc. among
them, in addition to solitaries and even recluses. But, in itself,
to be a Camaldolese does not necessarily imply the radical
decision of casting oneself exclusively on God.

THE RECLUSE. Materially, he or she enjoys a solitude that is
often profound. In fact, however, it is fragile and subject to all
manner of contingencies quite outside the recluse's control.
When one considers the life of a recluse in actual practice, he
or she always forms a part of a community of some kind, be
it monastic, canonical or parochial, and depends on it both
spiritually and materially. This means that his or her situation
is very unstable, even if it sometimes offers exceptionally
favourable circumstances.

BEYOND THE ABSOLUTE

Once admitted within the limits of a Charterhouse, we find ourselves right in the midst of Carthusian life itself. Now begin the surprises, even if we knew in advance that we would find ourselves at the heart of a community life. We came with the idea of isolating ourselves completely, and casting ourselves upon God alone. Now we find ourselves caught in the complicated network of obligations involved in family life. We thought to find ourselves surrounded by saints and, to our horror, discover a prevailing mediocrity. Even worse, we end up realizing that the Absolute has vanished within us: nothing remains of that for which we came. Does this mean that we have been sidetracked, or is it some new 'trick' of God, who is revealing himself in a way we did not expect?

Joining the family

When there are so few dwelling in the heart of the same desert, drawn by the same ideal, there is no question of living side by side as strangers. He who has no wish to join in the life of the family will be rejected by it and soon discover that his life in cell is radically undermined. If he truly wishes to persist in his search for the Absolute, there is no alternative but to accept this family life and to join it wholeheartedly, in loyalty and honesty.

This social dimension is quickly revealed as being at the very heart of Carthusian life. No one can find God while forsaking the road laid down in the Gospels, that is, the path of charity. It would be fruitless to seek the Absolute and, at the same time, seek to dispense ourselves in any way from love of our brothers. For the teaching of Jesus and of the beloved disciple is clear: the love which binds together the children of God is the very same love that unites the Father and the Son. To join the Carthusian family is to enter fully into the life of the divine family and, with the risen Jesus, to penetrate the veil and come into the presence of God. Yet, in a Charterhouse, this human image of the divine family seems limited and constrained and only makes sense when placed within the context of that great family of the children of God – the mystical body of Christ: his Church.

It is impossible to overestimate the mental adjustment often required of the young monk in this apparent reversal of values. Having come to lose himself in an Absolute which had totally overwhelmed him, he suddenly discovers this Absolute to be completely different from what he had imagined. The 'Absolute' is a way we have of imagining God: the reality of God is the Son who is in the bosom of the Father, and who revealed this reality to us when he said that the Father loved the Son, and that they both loved us and would come to us. In the end, it is a crucifying choice that we have to make: either the Absolute which contents us by enclosing us within ourselves, or the relationship that will open us to the infinite, but at the cost of wrenching us asunder and exposing us to all those around us, whatever affinity we may or may not have for them.

The kingdom of mediocrity
One does not need to spend very long in a Charterhouse to become aware that it is rampant with many petty problems and the presence of ordinary human weaknesses, even if everyone is doing his honest best to strive towards that perfection of which the Father is the supreme model. There is nothing new about this. Historical accounts of life in the Charterhouse, as well as the annals of the Order, show that individuals of great sanctity or distinction are very rare in our communities. The life of most Charterhouses is a dull sort of grey. One encounters disputes with neighbours and little incidents within the communities.

A deeper insight into souls gradually allows us to discover that behind these disappointing exteriors often lie real treasures of interior life, of generosity, and of an authentic search for God. Nevertheless, it cannot be denied that these precious gems are often buried in unattractive dress. How could it be otherwise, face to face with the Absolute? Is this not the price of such dangerous proximity to fire? For it highlights all our faults, all our roughness of character and all the petty misery which in other circumstances would be swallowed up in the surrounding sea of trivialities. To wish to come face to face with the light of God is deliberately to consent to expose all our faults and pettiness to the hard light of day. These first become apparent to others, and then, as we become enlightened, to ourselves. We first discover mediocrity in others and afterwards, in ourselves.

Risks are always involved when our aim is high. Seeing ourselves apparently ever more distant and removed from our goal is a painful suffering. On a more prosaic level, this mediocrity is the consequence of our separation from the world. To the extent that solitude is effective, it deprives us of a great many advantages which might introduce into the community an *élan* or a renewal which would mask the mediocrity or remedy it in some way. The critical choice must be made: either choose God and accept that perfection must come first and foremost from within, or leave open certain gates to the world so that certain means, other than those proper to the desert, play a part in one's life. The usual choice in the Charterhouse is the former. To make such a decision quite deliberately represents a very real sacrifice – an entry into solitude at a very exacting price. In effect, it is a conscious decision to leave untapped a part of our human potential so that God may well up from within. Such conditions are only suitable for those who have already attained a certain level of human maturity and self-motivation in their spiritual and intellectual life.

Going beyond the Absolute

The discovery of mediocrity first in others and then in oneself is a step towards an even more disconcerting discovery. Holiness, perfection and virtue – all these qualities which, without realizing it, we believed to be reflections of the Absolute within ourselves – begin to vanish. Everything which tends to make the ego a point of reference or an autonomous centre must disappear in order to conform with the resurrected Christ who is but pure relation to the Father. Even his humanity is now endowed with divine names. All created riches have been stripped away in order to be nothing but pure relation.

Such is the direction which the monk must take little by little: first, in his interior life and then in all his activities, whether in cell or in community. He must learn never to focus on himself but to be taken up in the movement of a divine love which has neither beginning nor end, neither goal nor source, neither limit nor shape. He must surrender to the breath of the Spirit, without knowing whence he comes nor whither he goes.

These few reflections give some idea of the increasingly disconcerting discoveries that await us when we allow ourselves to be guided by divine light. Yet this evolution, which obliges us to go infinitely beyond what seemed to us in the beginning the most alluring ideal, is the work of God. He would seem to have deceived us, since he has drawn us where we had no wish to go, but, in fact, little by little he is unveiling a truth to us which we were unable to accept at the start. This *amen* of God is the Carthusian's sole guarantee, his only support in a journey which precisely entails his holding nothing back, and finding no longer in himself any wellspring of strength or autonomous judgement. He must only believe in Love and give himself up to it.

4

'And Jesus Took with Him . . .'

**Jesus took with him Peter,
James and John and climbed
the mountain to pray.**
                              (Luke 9:28)

Jesus climbed the mountain in order to pray. The Transfiguration is in the first place a mystery of prayer, and more precisely, of the prayer of Jesus himself. He is called by the Spirit to meet his Father more intimately in solitude. There are numerous passages in the Gospel which show how solitude and prayer are for the Lord closely connected. He goes to pray in solitude; when he wishes to pray he withdraws into solitude.

Jesus climbs the slopes of the mountain as did the great men of prayer of the Old Testament who were called by God to meet him and see him face to face. Moses and Elijah had experienced the most glorious moments of the Old Covenant when the Lord had revealed all that could be understood of his name before the coming of the Son.

Jesus goes off into solitude and yet he does not go alone. He chooses three companions. Unlike Moses and Elijah, Jesus is not to present himself in isolation before the Father. The former represented the whole of Israel; yet it was for a totally solitary encounter that they went to meet the Almighty. In the economy of love, it is no longer the same: the solitary prayer of Jesus is at the same time a prayer of communion. He takes with him the three confidants whom we will find a little later in another solemn moment of prayer in Gethsemane. Jesus has need of a fraternal presence at his side. He does not wish to be, nor can he be, alone. The prayer of the disciples is not even mentioned, for there is only one prayer: the prayer of Jesus. Their role is simply to be united to him, their hearts beating to the rhythm of his.

Jesus climbed the mountain in communion with his brothers, and yet we cannot fail to see how he is separated from them. They fall asleep. Peter, full of his usual good will, cannot help making a suggestion which one realizes at once makes no sense. When Jesus asks them to keep silent until the Resurrection, they can only ask: 'What is "Resurrection"?' Jesus is, therefore, truly alone even if his disciples are physically present and even when, with all their hearts, they wish to be near him.

Let us consider this profound balance of solitude and communion which characterizes the prayer of Jesus. Up in the mountain, away from the crowds, he is with his disciples; while close to them, he nevertheless enters into a deeper solitude where no one can follow him. The prayer in the Garden of Olives will give a yet more poignant witness of this interaction of presence and absence which defines our prayer of communion.

In the Transfiguration, we are dealing with exceptional prayer. The Spirit of the Lord is upon Jesus. As at his baptism, he must enter into a solemn moment of his return to the Father. The Transfiguration is a pinnacle of his existence, yet it is much more a point of departure. Jesus enters thus into the mystery of his 'exodus', as St Luke says in reference to the conversation between the Saviour and Moses and Elijah. The Paschal Mystery is already beginning, and is played out in light, just as in Gethsemane it will be played out in darkness. Jesus is at the summit of a new Horeb, flooded by the Spirit; he is in the process of concluding the new alliance which will soon be sealed in his blood. The light in which he is bathed reveals his full right of access to the Father. It inaugurates already his entrance into glory.

However, this meeting of the humanity of the Son with the Father does not take the form of a crushing presence on the part of an impersonal God. It appears rather as communion with Moses and Elijah. His two predecessors on the holy mountain are there to welcome him and to show that the New Covenant

is a work of love. There is not only the communion of the
Father and the Son in the Spirit; there is its permanent and
visible sign: the encounter between human beings of flesh
and blood who, when transformed by light, continue to possess
a heart that thirsts to give itself.

We have spoken up to now of the prayer of Jesus, for it is at
the centre of the mystery of the Transfiguration. Yet we cannot
pass over in silence the presence or, better still, the contemplation of the disciples.

They form a group profoundly united. Since the distant day
when Jesus called them from their fishing nets at the edge of
the lake of Genesareth, to journey with him through Galilee,
they had entered into intimacy with the Master, and it is this
common bond with him which sealed a unity among them that
reaches its zenith at this time.

Did they realize what was going to happen? It is not likely,
judging from the naïveté of their reactions. They climbed the
mountain with him; but, as we have said, we cannot speak of
a prayer which would be strictly theirs. They are simply
engulfed in the radiance of Jesus. Their contemplation does
not spring from their own depths, but is an overflow of the
prayer of Jesus which descends on them. Today, 'God himself
has shone in their hearts to radiate the knowledge of his glory,
the glory on the face of Christ' (2 Corinthians 4:6).

We should see in them much more than simple witnesses:
they truly participate in the mystery which is being
accomplished before their eyes, in so far as they receive what
Jesus gives them in simplicity and humility. God is content with
this good will; even as Peter makes a remark which betrays his
lack of understanding of the situation, the cloud through which
they will enter into intimacy with the Father is already
approaching.

'A bright cloud covered them with its shadow.' We find here
the hallmark of the most solemn moments in salvation
history, when God chooses to reveal his greatest secrets. On
Sinai, Moses entered into a cloud before Yahweh revealed his
name to him. In like manner, at the dedication of the new
temple, Solomon found himself taken up into a cloud as
Yahweh came to take possession of his dwelling place. Finally,

at the Annunciation, is this not the characteristic sign of the
presence of God that the angel gives to the Virgin: 'The Holy
Spirit will come upon you and the power of the Most High will
cover you with its shadow'?

Here, then, are the three poor disciples, men of no exceptional merit, who enter into the cloud, the loftiest image of
divine power. They have direct access to the Father, for they
are close to Jesus and are his friends. Their dullness, their
incomprehension, does not matter, their hearts are given totally
to Jesus and that is enough.

They are to become sharers in the glory which suffuses Jesus.
What occurred in the depths of his soul is made known to them
by the Father's voice. He reveals once again that Jesus is his
Son, the Beloved, the Chosen One of whom the prophets spoke.
The occasions on which the Father himself proclaims his intimacy with the Son in the Spirit so directly are extremely rare
in the Gospel. The baptism of Jesus was the first time; Peter at
Caesarea Philippi had spoken in the same way under the direct
inspiration of the Father; now today, on the mountain top, the
Father again intervenes to make the disciples penetrate more
profoundly into the mystery of the Son, the Son who enters
into the Paschal Mystery so as to return to his Father.

From now on, the disciples will be bearers of a momentous
secret. They had followed Jesus into a mountain solitude in
order to pray near him; now they are introduced into a solitude
still greater: the solitude of mystery. They were told by the
Father to listen to Jesus, but he has nothing to say to them for
the moment other than to keep quiet. Solitude in the company
of Jesus has introduced them to silence.

Henceforth they carry in their hearts this vision which will
stay with them to the end of their days: 'We saw his glory, the
glory that is his as the only son of the Father, full of grace and
truth' (John 1:14).

But already the cloud has passed. 'Arise, do not be afraid.'
They are astonished: Jesus is alone; there is silence . . . life
continues.

The lessons that one can draw from the Transfiguration concern every Christian; but we can easily see in it a call to a
better understanding of our vocation in its deepest aspects. To

conclude, let us summarize the important features of this spiritual doctrine.

Solitude is the place of prayer. The only true prayer which radiates there is that of Jesus: all other prayer is a reflection of the light which shines forth from his face. Let us, therefore, follow Jesus in solitude, relying only on the power of his call; it is not our competence or our virtues which give us access to the Father, but the invitation of Jesus to follow him up the mountain.

The solitude of prayer is equally a place of communion. Jesus has called us; we are with him. Yet we are all brothers united in the love which he lavishes upon us in a single movement of his heart. It is not in isolation that we climb the holy mountain, but as brothers whose solitude is fraternal.

At the heart of this communion, however, a new form of solitude exists. Jesus prays apart and seems not to communicate with those around him. It is at the heart of this deeper solitude that a more intimate communion is revealed: a communion coming from God, manifested in different ways, but always the sign and reality in us of the communion among the Divine Persons.

Such is our ideal: to enter into the Paschal Mystery with Jesus and to receive from the Father the revelation that his Son has been given us and is ours to welcome. We have no other call here below than to bear this mystery, in silence, in our heart. Amen.

5

*Einsam und Gemeinsam**

The other in my prayer.

Solitude is the reply to a call from God to encounter him alone. It would seem that to let oneself be driven by such an aspiration would be to transcend every human being. Yet, the day that one finds oneself truly in the presence of God, one suddenly discovers that it is impossible to enter into contact with him without becoming like the one who, by essence, is a God-who-is-given.

Within himself, God is the mutual gift offering of Person to Person. How could we hope to become like him in any way, if we are not equally open with all our being to an unlimited reciprocal gift?

But Jesus taught us by his teaching and by his life that God was equally outside of himself, given without limit to whoever is capable of receiving him. He is a God given to everyone, that is to say, to my neighbour, to each person whom my love can reach. How could I then present myself before the Lord if, on my part, I have not done all that I could to become someone who gives of himself?

The other is thus necessarily present between God and myself, because present in God and present in me. My encounter with God and his with me are conditioned by my attitude towards the other, by everyone who enters into my existence as a solitary. In this respect, two attitudes are fundamentally possible: either evasion, refusal, denial, forgetting and ignoring,

---

*'Alone and together'

or else, on the other hand, full acceptance, a conscious effort to take him or her into account, to allow the other to penetrate into our very depths through love, to love unconditionally.

We are now in a realm where we cannot be satisfied with words; there is no one else to fool, especially not ourselves, because we are in the light of God. Accepting the other is not at all a matter of appearances but of the most intimate and concrete reality. It is I myself, in my most authentic solitude, with all my narrowness, weakness and fragility that must accept the other, whoever he or she may be, as he really is, with all his limitations, faults, shortsightedness, etc. From the depths of my heart, I must accept his presence, not as though he were an intruder or a stranger, but as a sort of absolute that is the very condition of my existence in the eyes of God as his son. I cannot be the likeness of God if I am not fully possessed by the other, if I do not let myself be fully possessed by him. My whole heart must belong to him, or, at least, I must place it at his disposal and expose it to all the risks that this entails.

To welcome the presence of the other in this manner does not only mean agreeing to bear him within my heart in silent recollection, but also adapting myself to the concrete require-ments of everyday existence, in the presence of such and such a person, and being thus obliged to consent to all sorts of things not to my liking, that may even separate me from a certain interior image I have of God, or disturb and annoy me. All this, obviously, within the limits of the existence that the Lord has wished for me.

Nevertheless, the essential attitude of the solitary is to accept the presence of the other in the very depths of his heart. In that way he will be able to present himself before the Loved One perfectly, at one with himself, at last freed from himself, being nothing more than perfect openness to God. Far from being a source of division or dispersion, this availability toward the other enables us to leave the realm of unlikeness for a region of untainted similiarity to God.

The goal may seem a distant one, but we should never lose sight of it at the risk of imagining that we have already entered into solitude, whereas we remain reserved and reticent, and more or less openly refuse to welcome the least of our brothers.

Perhaps it would not be superfluous to consider more closely the possibilities we have of refusing the other, in order to unmask the devious ways of nature or of the Devil.

The most extreme attitude is that of flight, of evasion: we run from others, since we consider them an obstacle between God and us. Their presence bothers us; their faults weigh us down; they do not understand our ideal; their own life seems derisive to us. Suppose that all these judgements are true. Even so, the person of my neighbour always remains worthy of respect, of welcome and of love. Nothing, absolutely nothing, should prevent me from loving him with a love that comes from God in Christ; nothing, neither principalities, nor powers, nor any other creature.

Another way to proceed, apparently more noble, consists of allowing others to enter into our solitude since we are men and Christians, and therefore, inseparably bound to one another, but once this concession is made, we relegate them to a region of our heart which they have no right to leave; once again we erect a wall between them and us. In the end, we arrive at the same result as that mentioned earlier. I seek dialogue between myself and God, but others have only the right to be passive and un-useful spectators. When all is said and done, I still consider them as obstacles or at least as superfluous objects.

We can also assume the other into our prayer in a way which, though certainly good in itself, still implicitly creates a separation between him and us. We agree to give him a place in our heart, but with the intention of changing him, of reducing him to dimensions that suit us. We still consider him in what seem to be his differences, his opposition to us; we have not given ourselves totally to him. To pray for others is certainly not to be condemned, but is this the form that God wishes it to take in him who has entered into solitude for him? Does he not rather expect the solitary first of all to love others as the heavenly Father loves them, that is, without limitations or restrictions, sending them his Spirit who is good. The Spirit alone can know what each one is called to become.

As long as I maintain toward the other an attitude of division of any sort, I do not live in solitude because I am in dispute with him. I am not free as long as I have not abdicated my

independence before him, in order to be possessed only by the
Spirit of Love. I will truly enter into solitude only the day when,
by God's grace, I will have become sufficiently like him for the
other to be no longer in any way a cause of dissimilarity between
the Lord and me. God is my solitude, but how can I enter into
God if I have not made my heart like unto his?

These considerations oblige us to enlarge our perspectives
and to realize that the solitude pleasing in the eyes of God is
not merely that of the soul withdrawn into the desert, but
primarily, the solitude of the one who has found God through
opening his heart to others. He who leads neither the contemplative nor the solitary life, but who has learned how to
render his whole being available to the love of his brothers, is
nearer to divine solitude than he who has enclosed himself in
a cell in order to ruminate bitterness and foment discord with
his brother.

6

Learning to Listen*

They found him in the Temple,
sitting among the teachers,
listening to them and asking
them questions.

(Luke 2:46)

My dear friend,

The Presentation of Jesus in the Temple is the first of the many visits that the Son of God made to his Father's house during his life, before becoming himself the supreme Temple of the presence of God on earth. In the Scriptures, the Temple never seems to be considered as the place of prayer for Jesus, but rather as the place of the word, and the place in which to listen. On this first occasion he is there as a little, silent child; but immediately afterwards, the Gospel shows him to us as the young adolescent listening to the elders and letting himself be taught by them. During his public life, he was the one who taught, in season and out of season, trying to open the ears of the Jewish people.

As you begin your religious life, I would like to draw your attention to this example of our Saviour whose will it was to be taught and formed by men, whereas, later on, he himself would find it impossible to have a hearing among them. We will try to see how the monastic life you are embracing today is also an experience of listening. We, too, put many obstacles

---

*Sermon given on the Feast of the Presentation of our Lord, for a Clothing ceremony.

in the way, and it is only by earnestly seeking to encounter Christ, and ardently pursuing this aim, that you will succeed.

First, let us take a brief look at what the Statutes have to say on this. They insist several times on the fact that solitude is not an end in itself: the aim of solitude is to allow us to hear God within us. This is an important theme that we find repeated in many different forms: we are to stand listening like the prophet on Mount Horeb; we are to converse with the divine Word; to leave all the doors of our soul open to God so that he may silently enter in; we are to be like a peaceful lake, having become by silence a pure reflection of Christ, etc. These different images are all trying to teach us the same thing: in the words of Sister Elisabeth of the Trinity, we have to make ourselves completely *enseignable* – 'teachable'. We are to be free within; our souls are not to be cluttered up with noise and sterile activities, but attentive and ready to detect the signs, sometimes so delicate, of the presence of the Lord speaking to our heart.

The preparation for listening to God is listening to others. The Statutes insist on the quality of welcome we are to offer our brothers when we have occasion to converse with them or relate to them: we must know how to listen to them, and understand them with both heart and mind; we are to go beyond mere appearances, and not allow ourselves to be troubled by the different ways they may have of approaching the same questions. So the Statutes give us a whole pedagogy of what it means to listen. Listening to others is not the aim of our life, to be sure, but welcoming our neighbour in this way will train our hearts to become silent, in order to be ready to receive the secret of the Other. For, in whatever circumstances, our main concern must be not just to receive some message or other, but, through the message, to discover the depths of the heart of the one who is speaking to us. If we are not able to do this with the brothers we can see, how will we be able to do it with God whom we cannot see?

These are only brief indications, but enough for you to see how this touches on the very heart of our life of solitude. This solitude does not consist in shutting ourselves away between four walls in order to cut ourselves off; or refusing to welcome others; or trying to be alone with ourselves at all costs.

On the contrary, solitude is the privileged place for listening, a place of silence: so, not a place of emptiness, but of communion with a reality which cannot be expressed in words. Normally, then, it is with joyous enthusiasm that we set off to master silence and the art of listening. However, experience shows that the results often fall short of our expectations.

For, after this summary of the teaching of our Statutes, we have to be well aware of the obstacles, coming from deep down in our innermost selves, that we oppose to a genuine attitude of listening to the Other, whether it be the Lord himself or our brother.

This is evident, and sometimes in a rather sad and humiliating way, in the exterior relations we have with one another in daily life. First there is the liturgy, an action accomplished in common, and so involving a continual listening to others in order to harmonize with them in voice and heart; then there are the conversations we have, either between individuals or in common, during recreations or walks; there are all the many little occasions of helping one another or reacting in the presence of a brother. Experience proves that in these matters we are subject to what could be called the deformation of solitude.

Spontaneously, each of us gets used to living isolated in his cell with no obstacles to his desires, no one else's thoughts to contend with, no need to adapt to opinions differing from his own. This results in a tendency for each individual to be enclosed in himself. At every level, we remain confined to the limits of our own little world. We are absorbed in our own particular devotions; our reflections always return to our pet ideas; everything is arranged according to our personal tastes; we have our own system for absolutely everything: it is a sort of systematic organization of egoism in which we risk being engulfed.

This results almost automatically in our putting on a sort of mask when we are with others, so as to protect our little treasures. We become incapable of ever meeting anyone else. Our deepest self is carefully sheltered; it has not the slightest concern, nor the slightest desire, to come into the presence of the deepest self of our brother. What complications that would lead to! So there is a risk of relations remaining permanently on a very superficial level, with mutual agreement carefully to avoid annoying one another. I dare say the bond of charity is not actually violated, but how weak and superficial it can become, impaired by so many omissions and negligences.

This is a fact of experience, and obvious to all of us if we are lucid enough to look at what is happening within ourselves and around us. It is easy to draw the conclusions for our interior life. What meaning can our prayer have in such a setting? What real encounter can there be between the Word of God, the eternal Word, and someone who habitually lives shut away like this in such a well-camouflaged house?

Don't think that I am deliberately exaggerating the severity of the temptations that will assail you in your cell: it is of utmost importance for us to realize that we have to go beyond the human satisfaction that solitude gives us in order to open ourselves up completely to the light and truth which are not to be found in ourselves, but in forgetting and abandoning the self. It is only then that we can start speaking of solitude for God.

The picture I have just painted is alarming, and the temptation is to react not just with good will, but also very incompetently, with the idea that a good dose of attention, good will and perseverance will put things right. All that is certainly useful, but is not the solution. The real remedy is more radical and goes deeper: it is in a truly authentic encounter with Christ. He comes to you continually through the Scriptures, through his presence within you; his word is addressed to you personally and his Spirit is trying to penetrate into the depth of your spirit. Welcome them.

In his conversation with Nicodemus, Jesus gives us an example of what might happen to us too when we meet him. This teacher in Israel is full of wise theories, and confident in his own experience; as soon as Jesus starts talking to him seriously, he refuses to be drawn, or opposes objections which he thinks are irrefutable. In fact, he is not really listening to the Master. He is not accepting to be born again as Jesus is asking him to do. Yet that really is the only solution, if we want to see the Kingdom of God.

This is the true meaning of the solitude you want to embrace. Let go of human wisdom, calculated prudence, and your own little projects, so that you can be taken up into the light of truth. Implacably, this light will reveal all the cunning tricks and resistances that the 'old' man in you uses to defend himself and remain in control. You must accept to see him disappear if you really want to be born anew, and to receive a new life welling up from the depths of your heart, where God has always been present without your knowing it.

This is the teaching Jesus gives you in the Temple: you are to be completely at the service of the Father, ignoring all that is not him.

To end these reflections, I would like to entrust you to the Virgin Mary who accompanied our Lord Jesus on the first occasions when he went to the Temple. She, too, had to live through times of sorrow, when she discovered the total renouncement of all possessiveness with regard to her son that the Word of God required of her. He belongs to God alone. In this way she was being prepared to train you and guide you towards the dispossession of yourself and of everything except listening to the Father, and the birth of the divine Word in your heart.

My dear friend, these few reflections will give you an idea of the demands the Carthusian life will make on you. What do you think of them? Are you determined to continue in your project?

7

Solidarity of the Solitary

There is no escaping the obvious teaching of Jesus and of Paul: only real, concrete charity, lived out in a practical way, can lead us to God. How can this exigency be compatible with the solitude that we know, too, is a necessity for us? Let us not be too quick to answer that 'it suffices to have the love of your brothers in your heart and to pray for them.' Not only does this risk being too glib, but more importantly, we would be missing out on the profound nature of our vocation. We are not hermits; nor are we cenobites, living permanently in community. It is the harmonious association of these two vocations that constitutes what we can call the mystery of the Carthusian vocation.

Our role in the Church is to be *a communion of solitaries for God*. To be men for God: that indeed is the first call that the Lord has made to us. And to be solitaries for God: all the details of our life show this to be our way. But we are not isolated solitaries; we are in the desert in communion with brothers who share the same ideal as ourselves. The task which each brother is trying to accomplish, hidden in his cell or in the silence of his workshop, is one that he shares with all his brothers: that of being consecrated to God in solitude. It is this task, at once single and shared, which unites us (cf. 3.4). The communion this creates is visible at every level: just as much in material contingencies as in the intimate union of our hearts, or in our fraternal gathering around the Prior in one and the same 'Carthusian Church'.

This multiform communion, rooted in silence and solitude, is our greatest prayer. It is divine life shared among us in such a way that 'it is the unity of the Father and of the Son and of

the Holy Spirit which constitutes us persons gathered together
in unity' (cf. St Cyprian, *On the Lord's Prayer*). As this union
between solitude and community is the specific form of our
vocation, it must mark our prayer as such. We have already said
how, of its nature, this prayer is solitary and silent; let us now
see how it must also have the dimensions of a communion.

The first reaction of Christians, even those who have but
little knowledge of the contemplative life, is to consider us as
being deputed to pray for others. It seems quite normal to
Christians that we should be permanently interceding for them.
This spontaneous attitude is indicative of a function that the
Church has always recognized as ours. It is, so to speak,
the basic form of communion present in our prayer.

This aspect of our vocation was developed at length in the
Constitution '*Umbratilem*',* precisely in the perspective of co-
operation with the apostolic activities of the Church. This
teaching is taken up by the Statutes:

> Christ redeemed the human race from the oppressive bond-
> age of sin above all by pouring forth prayer to the Father,
> and by offering himself to him in sacrifice. Thus it comes
> about that we, too, even though we abstain from exterior
> activity, exercise nevertheless an apostolate of a very high
> order, since we strive to follow Christ in this 'the inmost
> heart of His saving task'. (34.4)

The Council declared also: 'Members of those communities
which are totally dedicated to contemplation . . . motivate the
People of God by their example: by imparting a hidden, apostolic fruitfulness, they make this people grow . . . They are an
overflowing fountain of heavenly graces' (*Perfectae Caritatis*, 7).

We find the same inspiration in the passages of the Statues
that invite us to keep informed about the great problems in the
Church, and the great movements in the world of today. The
aim of this recommendation is not to satisfy vain curiosity, but
to allow us to be in communion with the sentiments of Christ
himself. For praying for others is sharing in God's desire to

---

*The Apostolic Constitution of Pope Pius XI, on 8 July 1924, approving
the new edition of the Carthusian Statutes.

draw them to himself; it is also being in communion with those who in their suffering are calling out to God and asking him for help.

In view of this attitude of real concern that we must have for our contemporaries struggling with the countless difficulties of daily life, many Christians could be scandalized by another form of prayer: at times it may be that the best way of praying for others is to forget about them. When we accept the deep poverty of this latter form of intercession, are we really betraying the expectations of our fellow men, or are we not, rather, responding in an eminent way?

Let us read again the words of Paul VI to the Prior of the Grande Chartreuse in his letter 'Optimam Partem':

> It is in the interest of the Church that the Order of Carthusians should remain very much alive: that its members, wanting to give God the honour which is due to Him, continually devote their whole strength to adoring Him. Through this pure and single-hearted worship, the Order is not only giving a sure and most valuable support to Christian people, but it is giving great help to others too, who are seeking the road to life and are in need of divine grace. For contemplation and continual prayer must be considered as tasks of primordial importance, carried out for the good of the whole universe.

The Pope's teaching is clear: our task is to adore God, to contemplate him; if we are doing this in all truth, then we are fulfilling integrally our role of intercession. Is this not what Jesus had taught? 'When you pray, do not heap up empty phrases as the Gentiles do; for they think that they will be heard for their many words. Do not be like them, for your Father knows what you need before you ask him' (Matthew 6:7–8).

In the eyes of the Lord, giving a detailed explanation to the Father of all the needs we have been asked to present to him is not what matters; what matters is that we should stand before him with a pure heart, and with boundless trust in his tender love for his children. This attitude is no easy way out; it is far more reassuring to rely on our words or our activity than to have complete and blind trust in the love of the Father, known in faith. We should be the bearers of the poverty of mankind not by spelling it out, but by experiencing it, in the vivid awareness that we are in the presence of God with empty hands, and that we must count totally on him.

And finally, do we not find the Statutes pointing us in the same direction? 'Although we offer many prayers for specific persons, we trust that all our prayers may, by the mercy of God, benefit first of all the universal Church to the praise of the glory of God' (65.25). These are the concluding words of the Statutes, but they also express the deepest reality of our communion through prayer; everything that unites us to God is of value to the Church. It is also consoling for us, since every prayer in the Church of Christ becomes our personal treasure.

Thus it may be that we are sometimes drawn interiorly to pray for particular intentions; at other times, we will feel drawn to forget about these specific needs, in the conviction that every light coming from heaven shines on all the Church and on the whole of humanity. Yet, all of this does not exhaust the potential of prayer as communion. The example of Christ takes us further. In his sacrifice that we celebrate each day, he is not simply offering prayer for each and every one, or forgetting others in an act of adoration and praise. Christ identified himself with us in such a way that, through communion with his body and blood, we might be the members of his body; so that, when he presents himself before the Father, it would be each and every one of us who thus has access to the throne of grace.

We read in the Statutes:

> The Carthusian Church finds its source and support in the celebration of the Eucharist Sacrifice, which is the efficacious sign of unity. It is also the center and high point in our life, as well as the spiritual food for our exodus in solitude, by which, through Christ, we return to the Father. (3.7)

If this is so, the attitude of Jesus identifying himself with us must also, in a way, become the centre of our life. Prayer is communion, because through prayer we are in total solidarity with all our brothers.

The chapter on the order's task in the Church states in various ways that 'By devoting ourselves exclusively to God we exercise a special function in the Church' (34.1). Our prayer is the accomplishment of a public role that has been officially entrusted to us. This does not mean that we are civil servants comfortably carrying out our job; it means that we are the Church at prayer: our prayer is the prayer of the Church recollecting herself in silence and coming together in the presence of God. We bear within us the needs of the world. Our own weakness is the sign, only too visible, alas, of the weakness of all of humanity; our own sins make it easy for us to be in solidarity with the sins of the whole world; our confidence in God's love cannot be limited to what concerns us personally, for our faith teaches us that in Christ we are all one in our journey to the Father. This realization should exorcise every temptation to esteem ourselves superior to anyone else; our cry to God, and the grace we receive from him, have the dimensions of the Body of Christ in which all humanity is gathered into one, from Adam to the last of the redeemed.

In this way we share in the grace of the Church herself. She who is the perfect communion of the children of God entrusts us with the mission of speaking in her name, on condition that we agree to give up our individual boundaries. That is the meaning of our solitude; it allows us to reach out in Christ beyond the narrow limits of a group to all those, known and unknown, who, in their different ways, are seeking the face of God.

> Our life clearly shows that something of the joys of heaven is present already here below; it prefigures our risen state and anticipates, in a manner, the final renewal of the world. (34.3)

> Let us give thanks to God the Father, who has made us worthy to share in the inheritance of the saints in the light. Amen. (35.9, quoting Colossians 1:12)

8

The Incarnate Life: A Mystery of Welcoming*

The parents of Jesus brought him to Jerusalem to present him to the Lord.

Dear Brothers,

Today Mary and Joseph are coming to present their little child to God. The signification of their liturgical gesture certainly goes far beyond all that they can possibly imagine. For their little baby has now come to the first stage of a long journey which will one day bring him back to the bosom of the Father. Presenting Jesus was not simply an exterior rite: for placing the Son in the presence of his Father meant being sure that he would be accepted. Jesus would say, later: 'I came forth from the Father and I am returning to the Father.' He is absolutely sure that the Father will welcome him every time he comes to him.

Today the mystery is taking place in darkness, for this little child is not able to take part in it in the light. But a few years later, when the young twelve-year-old boy stays on in the Temple, it is precisely because he has received this flood of light showing him that he must be in his Father's house. In the Son's journey towards his total, definitive return to his source, there is a succession of different stages, showing each time a progression in the way the Father welcomes him. The Baptism

*Sermon given on the Feast of the Presentation of our Lord.

in the Jordan, and the Transfiguration are the most outstanding
events in this journey, leading up to the day when he would
have to enter into the great and definitive passage of the Passion
and the Resurrection. Let us try to meditate on the practical
consequences of this mutual welcome that becomes thus more
and more manifest in the relationship between the Father and
the Son.

How is it, in fact, that the Father is disposed to welcome the
Son into himself so freely, if not because the Son himself, in
all his being, is total welcome towards the Father? We can see
Jesus' total openness to the will of the Father reappearing time
and again throughout the Gospel as the still point in the depths
of his soul. All his activity can be summed up as a conscious,
deliberate, and loving dependency on what the Father is teaching him to do or asking him to undertake, and on what the
Father is showing to be pleasing to him.

But there is infinitely more. Jesus' welcoming of the Father
is not limited to what he has to do. As he advances in life, Jesus
assumes more and more this total dependency of his whole
being on the One who sent him. As Son of God, he is, in the
very depth of his being, pure receptivity of the Father. He is
nothing but that. And this is what he has to assume more and
more in his existence as Son of Man. Every stage at which
the Father welcomes him a little further into his intimacy,
corresponds, in Jesus, to a progression in his dependency with
regard to his beloved Father.

It is in this visible, tangible way, as Saint John will say, that
the reality of the mystery of the Trinity is placed before our
very eyes. In this man, living on our earth, the deepest secret
of God is made manifest: the secret that he came to reveal to
us, so that we might have a share in it. The Son receives himself
totally from the Father, and the Father is total welcoming of
the Son who returns to him in love. That is what we, in turn,
have to live. How can we respond to such a programme?

'As the Father has loved me, so too have I loved you,' Jesus

tells us: which means that just as the Father has welcomed
Jesus into himself, so also is Jesus ready to welcome us. But it
also means that we must welcome the Son of Man with our
whole being, if we wish to be welcomed by him. This then is
the question we have to ask ourselves: to what extent am I
really ready, in the concrete and practical detail of my life, to
welcome Jesus into myself? To answer this question, let us try
to take Jesus as our model. As we have just said, he was totally
open to do the will of the Father. That will be the visible sign
that we are genuinely disposed to welcome Jesus into our lives:
our fidelity to listen to his will, to accomplish it and to let
ourselves be guided by it blindly. Moreover, like the only Son,
we have to welcome God with our whole being, accepting to
be His children more and more every day. Being born of God
is not something that happens in an instant: it is the result
of a repeated welcoming of the gift that God makes to us of
himself, a welcome that we try to make more and more transparent, so that we may become in truth the children he has
engendered.

Being born again in God

It is a marvellous ideal, but how far removed from the way
we really live! What obstacles we oppose to this simple and
transparent welcome of Jesus into our lives! The first and most
radical of these obstacles is sin: the determined refusal to welcome God into our life and to be his children or, at least,
to be loving children. Then, apart from sin, there are those
innumerable, less visible, or secret little brakes that we put on
the divine life within us, depriving it of the freedom it needs to
make us capable of being fully welcomed by Jesus into his body.

So we must learn, consciously and gradually as Jesus did,
how to present ourselves before God, in order to receive him,
and, at the same time, to be welcomed by him. It is a long and
difficult pedagogy, which has to be put into practice daily in
our relations with our brothers.

'My commandment is that you should love one another as I
have loved you.' Jesus himself teaches us the secret. Just as he
is welcomed by the Father so are we to be welcomed by him;
and as he welcomes us, so are we to welcome our brothers.

Therefore, it is to the extent that all my being becomes a living welcome of each of my brothers, that I will begin to be ready to be welcomed by Jesus. So our programme is precisely that: to become a living welcome of our brothers.

We would have to read through the whole Gospel again, especially the Gospel of the Sermon on the Mount, in order to set out the detail of this programme: (do not judge; do not condemn; forgive, and forgive repeatedly the same fault committed against you by the same brother; do not refuse a service; if someone asks you to go a hundred yards with him, accept happily to go a mile with the one who is requisitioning you; and so on.) That is the welcome that the Gospel asks me to practise with regard to my brother, not just in extraordinary circumstances, but today, and at every moment, as the normal respiration of my Christian being.

Note that this is not some sort of rule, exterior to our lives, that Jesus might have imposed on us as a discipline. These directives, outlined so simply, are truly the substance of our lives as children of God. When I give my brother all rights to be welcomed within me, I am not according him a luxury; I am simply trying to live in truth as the child of God I am: that is, to be as welcoming as I possibly can, because that will make me ready to be welcomed in turn by God himself.

The other side of this exchange of divine life that we are to practise among us is the permanent inclination to allow ourselves to be welcomed by our brothers. It is so easy, in fact, to refuse myself to my brother, under the pretext of discretion or respect of others, whereas he is prepared to welcome me, or may even feel a profound need of doing so. Let us remember, for example, the strong words addressed by Jesus to Simon Peter: 'If I do not wash your feet, you can have no part with me.' That means: if you are not able to accept my being at your disposition, at your service, welcoming you fully and completely into my heart, what have we in common? Could we not often ask the same question among ourselves?

Why does it seem so extraordinary to us, and almost incomprehensible, that someone should welcome us into himself? Is it not because, on our side, we are incapable of accepting ourselves as we really are? This is indeed the last, and not the

easiest form of welcome that we must practise. For we cannot
simply be content with what we think ourselves to be, turning
a blind eye on our limits, our shortcomings and faults. The
situation is much more delicate, for we have to discover ourselves, in God's light, just as we are: that is, as God sees us,
and, to a certain extent, as others know us, without illusions.
How we would like to shut our eyes at this point, and refuse
to see this image of ourselves, which then becomes so blinding!
Nevertheless, I have to go through this experience of welcoming
my own self. How can I present myself before Jesus, if I am
only bringing along with me a fake personage? How can I
imagine creating a real, living contact between us if, in fact,
the reality of what I am is not what I am offering him? If I want
to enter into this chain of welcoming, I have to learn how to
welcome my own self, sometimes at the cost of harsh experiences. The first step of this difficult exploration is often to
recognize that I have not the courage to welcome myself, and
to know that I will have to turn to the Lord humbly admitting
my inability to do so. It is from this level of humiliating truth
that I can then gradually climb all the steps of the ladder of
welcomes that we have been talking about.

Reflecting on Mary

We cannot end these reflections without mentioning our Lady,
who has been present at the heart of the whole of our meditation. For what perfect welcome can there be on earth that
does not depend completely on the welcome that Mary offered
to her Son at the Annunciation, and at the Nativity: a welcome
that she extended all through his life, giving him unreservedly
complete liberty to be at home within herself, right up to his
last dramatic passage from this earth to the right hand of the
Father.

Holy Mary, Mother of God, obtain for us a welcoming heart.
Teach us how to accept ourselves; make us transparent to our
brothers so that we may receive, in your Son, the gift of the
Father.

II

Interior Prayer

9

The Facets of Silence

**What benefits, what divine delight,
the desert's silence brings to those
who love it!**
        (St Bruno's letter to Raoul)

St Bruno's letters, written with all the fervour of his heart, are, from beginning to end, a kind of indirect avowal of all that the Lord had granted him to discover. This is especially true of his impassioned praise, addressed to Raoul, of the benefits which the solitude and silence of the desert afford. 'Only those who have experienced it can know,' he says. Then, without any transition, he shows his friend the extent of his knowledge on the subject. St Bruno was a man of silence and had penetrated its secrets. Our Statutes, following our Father's example, hark back many times to the beauty of silence and to the sacred value it represents in our life. Let us be guided by them now as we listen to St Bruno giving us instruction on silence through them.

Keeping silence is not a spontaneous attitude: it demands a conscious decision on our part. In order to enter into silence, one must really want it, and above all know why one wants to keep silent. If we intend to become men of silence, we must pursue it with a sense of responsibility.

This is exercised at different levels. First of all, with regard to others: 'Love for our brothers should show itself firstly in respect for their solitude' (1.4.4–4.12.5). To each one of us is entrusted the external, and even internal, silence of those around us. Silence is seldom a purely personal affair. Our role with regard to our brothers is exercised in the first place *vis-à-vis* external silence; it depends on us whether our immediate environment is conducive to recollection or dissipation, by the care with which we see to it that our attitude radiates a concern for peace and silence. 'The places where they (the brothers) work, like those where they live, should be so arranged as to be conducive to interior recollection . . . it should be quite apparent that they are a home where God dwells and not mere secular buildings' (2.11.3). Our influence is also exercised in the number of words we address to them, and, perhaps even more so, in the quality of those words, so that they tend to recollection, and not to dissipation. 'If, by chance, we come to know something of events in the world, we must be careful not to pass it on to others; news of the world should rather be left where it is heard' (1.6.7–2.13.4).

This responsibility towards our companions, however real it is, remains the sign of an incomparably heavier responsibility that we are entrusted with in regard to all men. 'In embracing a hidden life we do not abandon the great family of our fellow-men; on the contrary, by devoting ourselves exclusively to God, we exercise a special function in the Church' (4.34.1). This means that the quality of our silence is not a private affair between God and us; a source of silence and divine intimacy should well up from our heart and flow out over the whole universe. We may sometimes complain about the noise that dissipates hearts in the world, but is it not partly our fault, in so far as we do not fulfil our function as sources of silence?

Our responsibility towards others takes on such proportions because, in the end, it is before God himself that we are accountable for the silence that is entrusted to us: 'Devotion to the Spirit dwelling within them . . . requires that they should weigh their words well and be watchful of the extent to which they speak' (2.14.4). The Lord's temple, which we ourselves are, cannot be profaned, above all if we know that God chose us personally in order to do him honour in this sanctuary. So it is in the presence of God himself that we ought to refine our sense of responsibility: 'Let each one, therefore, listen to the Spirit within him, and determine what he can admit into his mind without harm to interior converse with God'

(1.6.6–2.13.10). God, in fact, is silent: in that, he is our model. But in so far as that divine silence is profound, it leaves us free, with freedom of choice: 'Now, no longer a child, but a man, let him not be tossed to and fro and carried about with every new wind, but rather let him try to find out what would please God and do it of his own free will, enjoying with sober wisdom that liberty of God's children, concerning which he will have to render an account before God' (cf. 4.33.2).

Some complain at times that solitude would progressively maim them because it would not allow them to exercise their human responsibility. Is that not the sign that they are not yet truly committed to the pursuit of silence? When the Statutes ask us to avoid readings 'that could disturb our interior silence', they continue, 'Of course, this exhortation presupposes a mature mind that is master of itself, and knows how to embrace honestly all that follows from the best part that it has chosen – the part of sitting at the Lord's feet and listening to his words' (1.6.5–2.13.11). Such is our true human responsibility, as great and as compelling in the secret of our cell as if we had to exercise it in front of a multitude; it lies in the honesty with which we wish to be faithful to the commitments we have made and the extent to which we take ourselves seriously before God, who speaks to our heart.

We speak of entering into silence. But in what does the contemplative's silence consist? Is it merely the fall of an inert pebble into a gaping hole? Perhaps we do not always avoid the error of mistaking the true silence of prayer for something resembling that very physical comparison. In actual fact, silence calls for 'a tranquil listening of the heart, that allows God to enter through all its doors and passages' (cf. 1.4.2). Silence is a listening: not the feverish expectation of a word that would strike our ears or fill our heart, but a calm receptivity to him who is present and who works noiselessly in our inmost being. That is why it is said that our solitude 'is holy ground, a place where, as a man with his friend, the Lord and his servant often speak together; there is the faithful soul frequently united with the Word of God; there is the bride made one with her spouse; there is earth joined to heaven, the divine to the human' (1.4.1–1.12.1). Silence, in fact, combines the absence of words,

on the lips and in the heart, with a living dialogue with the
Lord. Let us not launch into long discourses on this subject,
but let us return to St Bruno's avowal: 'The fruit that silence
brings is known to him who has experienced it. God has led
us into solitude to speak to our heart' (1.4.11). That is silence:
to let the Lord utter within us a word equal to himself. It
reaches us, without our knowing how, without our being able
to delineate its precise contours; nevertheless, the very Word
of God comes and resonates in our heart.

That is why we can never be satisfied with mere silence of
the lips. This

> would however be merely pharisaical, were it not the out-
> ward expression of that purity of heart to which alone is it
> promised to see God. To attain this, great abnegation is
> required, especially of the natural curiosity that men feel
> about human affairs. We should not allow our minds to
> wander through the world in search of news and gossip; on
> the contrary, our part is to remain hidden in the shelter
> of the Lord's presence. (1.6.4–1.13.1)

In fact it is so easy to remain quiet in one's cell while allowing
the mind to wander. Who has not experienced it? In that case,
we are still far from silence, even if our lips are closed and our
hands idle. 'Our part is to remain hidden in the shelter of the
Lord's presence' (id.). Recollection not only requires a rigorous
control of the imagination: all our faculties of knowing and
conceiving must reduce their undisciplined and turbulent
activity. 'Intent, then, on the rich substance of truth rather than
the froth of words, let us scrutinize the divine mysteries with
that desire to know which both springs from love and in turn
inflames love' (1.5.2). Therein lies a great lesson in wisdom:
however lofty or sublime the activity of our intelligence may
be, it could not reach silence if it did not flow humbly into a love
that listens and ends by foregoing complete comprehension. 'In
solitude we read, not to be informed about the latest opinions,
but so that faith may be nourished in peace' (3.21.11). The
important thing, in fact, is not that an idea be new or brilliant;
what we hope for from it is that it be the source of greater light
about God, a light that is born of and in peace. Silence is

precisely that quality of listening that enables us to savour God without the necessity of saying new things.

Such attention to God can only be the fruit of a general pacification of our whole being. The uncontrolled passions that cut across our sensibility, the anxieties, the excessive joys: all that should progressively find the path of order, with the help of God, but also through all sorts of wise practices.

> By working with his hands, the monk practises humility; he also brings his whole body under control so as better to attain stability of mind . . . It sometimes happens also that the very weight of our work acts as a sort of anchor to the ebb and flow of our thought, thus enabling our heart to remain fixed on God without mental fatigue. (1.5.3)

Listening to the Lord is no longer then an activity of the intelligence or the sensibility, but a sort of communion of our whole being with the presence of him who sustains it and communicates life in love.

If, through the Lord's goodness and after long, persevering efforts, we succeed in stabilizing this attitude, we will be close to that solitary soul which has become 'like a tranquil lake, whose waters well up from the purest sources of the spirit and, untroubled by news coming from outside, like a clear mirror reflect one image only, that of Christ' (2.13.15). Such is the 'last word' in the dialogue that God wants to maintain with us: to transform us into the very simple image of his own Son.

True silence is not the flower of a day that is picked at the outset. It is a fruit that ripens as the prize of long and costly efforts. Above all at the beginning, to be silent involves downright hard work, because it goes against our nature's spontaneous tendencies, to which we have the habit of yielding. 'If we are faithful, there will gradually be born within us of our silence itself something that will draw us on to still greater silence' (1.4.3–2.14.1). On certain days, we need courage to commit ourselves to the way of silence. We know that it means introducing the sword into our interior: peace will only appear when its opponents have been expelled.

'The journey, however, is long, and the way dry and barren, that must be travelled to attain the fount of water, the land of

promise' (1.4.1–2.12.1). The images used by the Statutes could
seem disheartening, but they are not excessive. Let us not start
out lightly on the way of true silence. It is a long and exacting
undertaking; it would be inhuman to want to strip ourselves
overnight of all sorts of habits that are ingrained in us. But it
would be dishonest to set out on such a path without being
firmly determined to traverse long distances with nothing to
quench our thirst. All sorts of exchanges with the outside,
which consoled us, must fade and disappear. Numerous inner
satisfactions, which diverted us and perhaps even gave us security, are also condemned to perish in the arid places to which
we deliver them. Israel in the desert, Jesus in his forty days, are
the models we must keep before us, not only in solitude, but
perhaps even more in our journey towards silence. We will have
no shortage of temptations and distaste. 'Let not the novice be
worn down by the temptations which are wont to beset the
followers of Christ in the desert; nor let him put his trust in
his own strength, but in the Lord who has called him and who
will bring to perfection the work he has begun' (1.8.13).

Ultimately, however, it is the Lord himself who will be the
heaviest trial to bear, if we agree to follow him to the heart of
silence. 'He cannot attain to this repose except at the cost
of stern battle; both by living austerely in fidelity to the law of
the Cross, and willingly accepting the tribulations by which
God will try him as gold in the furnace' (cf. 1.3.2). In fact,
who could affront God's silence without getting burnt by the
consuming fire that he himself is? To enter into silence is, in
fact, to meet God in his own house: doubtlessly a fine ideal,
but formidable in the transformations it must effect in us. Yet,
how could one not aspire to that goal, knowing that 'having
been cleansed in the night of patience, and having been consoled and sustained by assiduous meditation of the Scriptures,
and having been led by the Holy Spirit into the depths of his
own soul, he is now ready, not only to serve God, but even to
cleave to him in love?' (id.).

The ardour of the combat we have evoked has meaning only
if it is founded on a robust humility. The first sign it will give
us of its presence is the modesty with which we purport to
arrive at silence. The latter is not within our immediate reach;

we must have the humility of perseverance: 'It is good for a man to await the salvation of God in silence', Jeremiah already said; Guigo completed that teaching by adding: 'The solitary will sit and keep silence, for he will lift himself above himself' (id.). In order to enter into silence we must remain patiently quiet, without pretence or vainglory.

The other indispensable, humble attitude is that which makes us consider true silence as a pure gift from God. Certainly, we should multiply our efforts with prudence and perseverance; but let us not delude ourselves: to want to reach silence all by ourselves would lead to self-destruction, without attaining the goal. 'God has led his servant into solitude to speak to his heart' (2.14.1). The starting point of our silence can only be God himself who calls; to want to establish recollection from our own resources would be to plunge into a foolish adventure. 'He alone who listens in silence hears the whisper of the gentle breeze that reveals the presence of the Lord' (id.). From the moment we realize the Lord is inviting us to follow him in that direction, we should make ourselves available, but, like Elijah on the summit of Horeb, it is neither in the wind nor in the earthquake nor in the fire that we will find silence. The latter will come upon us when it is born of God himself in the form of a gentle breeze.

Silence is the work of God; but, it is much more than that, as we said: it is God's word. There lies the ultimate root of the humility which must become our very element if we wish to discover the source of silence in our heart. The example of Mary at the Lord's feet should enlighten us: 'Let Martha bear with her sister, as she follows in the steps of Christ, in stillness knows that he is God' (1.3.9). Mary had truly entered into silence: beyond the words that Jesus uttered, she detected that he himself was the eternal Son. Her efforts were not wanting: she 'purifies her spirit, prays in the depths of her soul, seeks to hear what God may speak within her'. But that effort is not the measure of the result; the latter is of a different nature, which totally eludes a creature's grasp: 'Thus, she tastes and sees – in the slender measure possible, though but faintly in a dark mirror – how good the Lord is' (id.). Thus we will arrive one day, if God gives us the strength and gentleness for it, at the true silence which is far beyond all words.

10

Prayer: A Mystery of Silence

To 'make' prayer. The expression is strange since it suggests the idea of doing something, of obtaining a result, of producing or creating. There, one finds again the old temptation of Western contemplative thinking symbolized in the juggler of Notre Dame. The story is touching in so far as it shows us that God hardly pays attention of what one does for him, since he sees the heart and not the deeds. Therefore, it is sad to see that the poor juggler little realized that it was enough to let his heart rest in the presence of the Lord in order to give him the very best. He had to do his juggling. It was not our Lady who needed to see him dance, it was the juggler himself who needed to do something. It was for him a matter of 'making' prayer.

It is not a question of 'making' prayer or even of making silence. Silence is not contrived. When one comes before the Lord with the mind full of images, with strong emotions and one's thoughts still in movement, one realizes the need for silence; the temptation then is to make silence. As if it were a question of clothing oneself in silence, of throwing over all the inner murmurings a cape which would hide or smother it. This is not to be silent; it is rather to cover up the noise or shut it up within ourselves, so that it is always ready to emerge at the slightest opportunity. There is no need to create silence or to inject it from without. It is already there and it is simply a matter of letting it rise from within us so that it eliminates by its very presence the noise that distracts or invades us. Silence can be mere nothingness: the silence of the stone, the silence of the mind numbed and deadened by its involvement with the material and exterior. This is not true silence. The only silence that counts is the presence of him who is no-thing.

Does not prayer often mean returning gradually and simply to true silence? Certainly, not by doing anything or imposing some kind of yoke or burden on ourselves but, on the contrary, by letting all our activity subside, little by little, into that true interior silence that will begin to assert itself and resume its rightful place. Once we have heard this silence we thirst to find it again. We must, however, free ourselves from the idea that we can of ourselves reproduce it. It is there; it is always there even if we no longer hear it. Indeed, there are days when it is impossible to recapture it, for the mill of the mind is grinding and it is impossible to stop the workings of the imagination and the senses. Yet, silence does abide in the depths of our will as a peaceful and tranquil acceptance of the noise and disturbances that hinder our coming to serenity of mind. Normally, though, it should be possible by means of a certain physical and intellectual asceticism (breathing, posture, etc.) to calm the undisciplined impulses of the mind in order to achieve at least a little stillness. All the same, silence is more profound than all accepted forms of meditation: *lectio divina*, lights from the Lord that help us penetrate his mysteries, reflection on themes that merit our attention, etc. All this is good and helps us to approach the truth. It is all very necessary in its own time.

Silence, however, is deeper still and nothing can replace it. There are days when we must forego silence in order to give our spirit the nourishment it needs. Yet we must not become light-headed with the wine of a partial truth which becomes clear to us; our thirst is deeper still and aims at a truth as near as possible to absolute Truth. Only silence, even if it is darkness, draws us to total light. Indeed, even the work of God only reveals to us its riches if it is the bearer of silence. The Divine Office only achieves its balance when it breathes forth in the depth of our soul the silence contained in the eternal Word.

We cannot, therefore, do anything. There is nothing to give. God does not wait for us to give him little gifts. He has no use for bulls of wild rams; what he wants is the spiritual sacrifice of our hearts. Must we say, therefore, that if we have nothing to give that is outside of us, we must give our very selves? Not even that. He does not ask us to become agitated, to invent formulas or methods for offering ourselves. Besides, if we really thought about it, what could that possibly mean? To go out of ourselves? But that would be to lose ourselves, to renounce being ourselves, taking our soul in our hands and offering it to God. If it is then not a question of our making a formal offering, should we, therefore, be receiving a gift from the hands of God? Not that either. We do not receive a gift from God, whether little or great; it is God himself that we receive. Yet what does this mean? Does he come to us in regal splendour, arrayed in majesty? In reality, we know that when we are silent God does not speak to us, nor does he reveal himself in any way, and yet he gives himself.

God gives himself to me. Yet, we must be careful not to act like frogs and puff ourselves up in an attempt to become as big as God. The gift of God is not something foreign to us; in a way, it is not different from us at all. For God, to give himself to us is to give us to ourselves. He gives me my being as child of God, ever springing forth anew. Experience shows that silence brings us back to ourselves. The danger would be to turn in on ourselves, and find contentment in a sort of self-complacency. To be truly oneself is to drink deeply at the wellsprings of our being, or more exactly, to be the spring nourished and sustained at the heart of God himself. God creates us in love and it is our being that we receive from him in love. At one and the same time, we become ourselves and we receive God himself. In fact, we are God, not through pantheism or monism, obviously, but by shared sonship. God begets me even before I know or desire it; but he also gives me his Spirit who allows me to receive this gift, of which I cannot clearly say whether it is he or I myself. It is simply a question of being oneself, or better, of becoming oneself at every moment, together with the Son who, from all eternity, in one unchanging moment receives his being from the Father.

magic formula

We are asked, therefore, to establish a relationship, not to achieve an end, or to realize an objective or to reach a goal. The aim, if we must use this word at all, is rather to be free from every concrete goal which might seem to be its own justification. There is nothing other to hope for or aim at than developing a true relationship with God in which we depend unconditionally on him and do not seek any other support apart from him. The gifts of God are important no longer;

what we can get for ourselves has no more interest; only one thing really counts: to have a genuine relationship of love with God. This brings in no 'returns'. We do not seek to be enriched or to enrich others, even less to enrich God. It is a kind of all-inclusive relationship in which we lose all the limited goals in which we are continually tempted to find our security. Thus, not only our mind and our activity, but our very being risks finding itself cut off from what gives it pleasure in life. Nevertheless, is there anything in these comforts which can still appear interesting or worthwhile, when compared with this supreme luxury of being pure dependency, nothing but the begotten of the Father?

Nonetheless, it would be wrong to believe that we can attain this attitude of dependence in its purest form by distancing ourselves from creation. On the contrary, it is only by passing through a creature that we can enter the heart of God. The pure relatedness of which we are speaking is, in fact, the establishment of a relationship of dependence on the risen Christ: the Man-Jesus, Son of God not only by birth but by the power of the Spirit who raised him from the dead to take his place as Son at the right hand of the Father. By his very being, he is the one who depends on the Father, and on whom we depend. The Paschal mystery is precisely the crucial moment in which his humanity, in giving itself to us without reserve, found itself in a state of complete dispossession which enabled him to be fully receptive to the Father, to receive the name above all other names.

There is, therefore, a presence of Jesus in the Spirit which is at the heart of all true prayer. It is not necessarily a felt awareness, but a real correspondence between his heart and ours, between our humanity, its flesh and blood earthiness, and the humanity of the Son of Man who through the Resurrection assumed the creation in its fullness and dominion over the universe. Prayer is not, then, an elegant stroll along the high places of the spirit, but, as was said above, a return to the deepest source of our entire being; flesh, soul and spirit. This source is the Divinity which comes to us in the Spirit sent by the risen Son from the bosom of the Father.

Benedictus Deus

11

The Prayer of the Heart

You have asked me to tell you about the prayer of the heart. I was asked about this several years ago but replied that I was reluctant to discuss a subject with which I was insufficiently familiar. With the passage of time I have gained some experience from observation of others and through things I have discovered in the course of my personal quest for our Lord. I will, therefore, confide to you some of my thoughts on the subject but would ask you not to attach too much importance to them.

You know that the prayer of the heart is the fruit of lengthy experience in the spirituality of the Eastern Church. What I am going to say certainly has points in common with that tradition, but I am very well aware of my too personal involvement when I describe it. Perhaps what I will say does not relate to the true prayer of the heart.

My intention is not to outline a rigid or permanent framework: it is more a pointing out the way to you, the path to follow, which one takes, however, without knowing exactly where it leads. The prayer of the heart is not a goal in itself. It is a way of life, a method of becoming attentive to God's voice within, and of making progress.

Before reading what I have to say, please first of all pray to the Spirit of our Lord that he may enlighten us both, because my only wish is to help him to bring light into our hearts.

ABBA, HALLOWED BE YOUR NAME

FATHER

When I pray, I do not call on the God of philosophers nor even, in a sense, on the God of theologians. I turn to my Father or rather, our Father. To be more precise, I turn to him whom Jesus, in complete intimacy and confidence, called Abba. When the disciples asked our Lord to teach them how to pray, he simply replied: 'When you pray you say: "Abba" . . .' To name God thus is to have the certainty that we are loved; a certitude of a different nature from that referred to by scholars but one derived from innermost conviction: a certitude of faith at which we have arrived, it seems to us, after periods of reflection, meditation and consideration of our interior inspirations; though ultimately this certitude is a gift. We have complete faith in the love we have in our hearts because it is the Father who has sent us his Spirit, now that his Son has entered into his glory.

It is because the Father loves me that I am able to turn to him in complete trust and confidence. I do not turn toward him to stress my virtues, nor for well-calculated reasons, but trusting in the infinite tenderness of the Abba for his Son Jesus, since he is also my Abba.

Jesus died for calling God "Father."

He is Father. What does this mean? He gives us life. He gives it not as he would give something separate from himself. He gives it just in giving himself. The only gift he can make is himself, his Person, and the outcome of that gift is a Son. A Son whose love for him is infinite. A Son for whom he has nothing but tenderness and who, in return, is nothing but tenderness for his Father.

That is the Father to whom I turn: the only one who can give me life, a perfect life in his own image. He wishes me, here and now, to be in his own likeness, not as if it were some kind of overlaid veneer but because he begets me by giving me a share in his own divine nature. That is what I mean when I ask him: 'Abba, hallowed be your name: that you should be your own very self, Abba, in me; that your name "Father" be realized perfectly in the relationship which is established between us. Abba, I ask you to be my Father, to beget me in your image and likeness purely out of love, that I, in return, through sheer graciousness on your part, may become tenderness towards you.'

The prayer of the heart consists simply in finding that path which will enable me to achieve, *vis-à-vis* the Father, that attitude which will enable him to sanctify his name within me. In me and in all his sons. In his only Son, consisting of the only One and all his brothers.

To pray is to welcome the Father and partake of the life he has given us through his grace. To welcome the Father is to allow him to beget his son and give birth to his kingdom in my heart.

TO SEE WITH THE HEART

What path are we going to take which will lead us to that meeting with God to which we aspire? What means are at our disposal to achieve this? Is it intelligence or an ability to learn and reason? Listen to the reply of Jesus: 'I give praise to you, Father, Lord of heaven and earth, for although you have hidden these things from the wise and the learned, you have revealed them to the childlike. Yes, Father, such has been your gracious will' (Matthew 11:25–26). That is what is so astonishing: the road is closed to the learned, to those who calculate and reason. It is not to them that God has revealed his secrets. But after all, has not God given us our heads, our ability to reason, to describe things and portray them, as a means of making contact with others? These faculties have certainly been given us by God. They are worthy ones; they are essential. While recognizing their limitations, let us not disdain them.

Yet, when I turn over a problem in my mind, or, more precisely, when I consider someone very close to me, and do so with my head rather than my heart, I distance myself from that person. I think about him or her, doing so from different angles in order to analyse at my leisure, but without committing myself.

In fact, I make no commitment; I keep my own security; I maintain my distance from that person. While doing all I can to understand him or her, I do not allow myself to become involved or touched by the inner force emanating from the heart of that person. Perhaps in some instances, such an approach is a good one. If I wish to love, however, that is certainly not the way to go about it.

Jesus continues: 'All things have been handed over to me by my Father; no one knows the Son except the Father, and no one knows the Father except the Son and anyone to whom the Son wishes to reveal him' (Matthew 11:27).

'All things have been handed over to me by my Father.' To be precise, this means that all distance between Father and Son has been abolished. Neither of them has sought to maintain his own security in the face of the other. They have accepted the challenge of committing themselves to each other completely. Thus can they know each other with that knowledge inspired by love which is presented as a mystery only the initiated can grasp. 'No one knows the Son except the Father, and no one knows the Father except the Son.' No one knows because no one opens his heart. If we wish to know the Father, we must be willing to accept this knowledge from the Son, who will reveal him to the extent that he sees that our heart is ready to welcome him.

In order to know God really, I must renounce my own security. I must eliminate that distance which reason and imagination have allowed me to create between him and me. I must realize how vulnerable I am, and bring out into the open that vulnerability which I have hidden so well. I must accept it as part of my being and allow the true feelings of my heart to take charge. Then, and only then, will it be possible for me to enter into a relationship with the Father and the Son, and as well, with all my brothers and sisters.

This means, concretely, that I must live on the level of my heart. I must give my heart the right to its own existence, to reveal itself as it will and to express itself in its own way, i.e. with the deepest of feelings – confidence, joy and enthusiasm, but also fear and sometimes anguish and anger. This does not mean living on the level of superficial sensibility. On the contrary, it means accepting that profound currents well up within us and lead us to an authentic encounter with our brothers and sisters.

That is what it means to be 'a little child': he who reacts with spontaneity and allows himself to be enveloped by the love of the person before him. How difficult it is for us to have the courage to be as children!

These reflections are in line both with the Gospels and with psychological development. The two areas are clearly distinct but complement and interpenetrate each other. We must learn to see everything with the loving regard of Jesus, not only created realities but also the Divine Persons. This is what I call 'seeing with the heart': to accept that the Son reveals the Father to me at the one level at which I am able to assimilate this revelation – the level where, by virtue of my human nature, there can be found within me an image of the intimate communion that exists between Father and Son: the level of my heart.

PURIFICATION OF HEART: PURIFICATION OF ONE'S WHOLE BEING BY THE HEART

There is no need to have a wide experience of human life, and even less so of the spiritual life, in order to realize that we are prisoners of a world almost boundless in its disorder – sin, emotional unbalance, open wounds, unwholesome habits, etc. All this renders our heart impure.

We noted above that the language of our heart is that of the emotions. All the confusion of which I speak leads to uncontrolled emotions; we give vent to them without being aware of them; they rule our conduct and create divisions within us;

they turn us away from God; they lead us into a kind of auto-mated evil life. And all this comes from the heart!

'What comes out of the mouth proceeds from the heart, and this defiles a man. For out of the heart come evil thoughts, murder . . . These are what defile a man' (Matthew 15:18–20). If I wish to rid myself of the contamination in my heart, first of all I must purify it.

Facing up to the urgent need to remedy this condition, it is usual to have recourse to what might be called traditional asceticism. This is a well-proven method adopted by many generations of monks, by Christians, by men and women of good will determined to free themselves from the bonds that hold them prisoner. It is a method which summons all the resources of our will power, our energy and our perseverance, illumined by faith and love. This asceticism has its merits and we should never cease resorting to it. Yet it also has its limitations.

In particular, as regard true purification of heart, we must reach out beyond these purely human techniques. Let us once more read what St Bruno had to say to his friend Raoul on the subject:

So, what do you think ought to be done, dear friend? What else, but to trust in the exhortation of God himself, and to believe in the Truth which cannot deceive? For he calls out to everyone, saying, 'Come to me, all who labour and are heavy laden, and I will give you rest' (Matthew 11:28). Is it not, after all, a most ridiculous and fruitless labour to be swollen with lust, continually to be tortured with anxiety and worry, fear and worry, fear and sorrow, for the objects of your passion? Is there any heavier burden than to have one's spirits thus cast down into the abyss from the sublime peak of its natural dignity – the veritable quintessence of right order gone awry?

Hence there is a type of purification in which, before any other endeavour, one must turn to Jesus and come to him in order to 'find rest'.

Christian Dad

After asking us to renounce being 'wise and understanding', Jesus issues us with an invitation to become as little children. To enter into the way of the heart is to realize that the only true purity is a gift of Jesus. 'Take my yoke upon you, and learn from me; for I am gentle and lowly in heart, and you will find rest for your souls' (Matthew 11:29). *(learn from Jesus)*

The fundamental purification starts the moment I take all the contamination and confusion with which I am afflicted and go to meet Jesus. This is not a task any easier than the traditional ascetic approach; but it is more effective, since it obliges us to live a life established in truth: the truth about ourselves, as it forces us to open our eyes to the reality of our state of sin; the truth about Jesus, who is truly the Saviour of our souls, not merely in a general and distant sense, but on the basis of direct contact with each and every one of the shortcomings with which we are afflicted. I have to learn, therefore, to offer up to him, without any reservation or afterthought, all the impurities of my heart, as they come to light, whether through the interplay of circumstance, or through some deep movement in my heart as it seeks to attain its real freedom at last.

Every time I discover one of these bonds which paralyse me, the most important thing is not to wage direct war against it, because in most cases I would feel satisfied with lopping off the branches without getting at the roots. What matters is to lay bare the roots and bring them into the open, however ugly and unpleasant they may be. It is a question of accepting them as they are, and of offering them up consciously and freely to the *"Love gift"* Saviour. In this way there is no risk that the classic prayer, 'Jesus, Son of the living God, have mercy on me, a sinner', be an ineffectual repetition. It is an acknowledgement ever renewed that another meeting is about to take place between the purifying heart of Jesus and my own polluted heart.

Clearly, in this process, an element of pure natural human psychology is present, but why should that be shocking? Does not the work of grace always build on nature? In the present instance, it provides a substratum for redemption, which effects a transformation in my heart, a healing of wounds, through a personal encounter with the resurrected Jesus. In this way we progressively acquire the habit of ever returning to him, especially with all that is confusing, obscure and disquieting within us.

This is an attitude of heart which is frightening at first. We have been told so often that we can offer up to the Lord only that which is good and beautiful; that we cannot bring to him anything which is not virtuous. Is it not a contradiction of the truth of the Gospels to say this? Jesus himself declares that he has not come for those who are well but for the sick. Hence we must learn, without false shame, to place ourselves before the divine doctor in all our misery, honestly admitting everything in us which is wrong, untrue and opposed to God. Only he can heal us.

MY BODY, MEETING PLACE WITH THE WORD AND TEMPLE OF THE SPIRIT

One is frequently tempted to interpret the conception 'prayer of the heart' in a symbolic way. To speak of the heart would be a figurative manner of evoking an interior, and therefore a spiritual, reality. This is wrong. All the movements of the heart, which are the mainstay of our relationship with the Father, are movements tied to our sentient, material being. We know from experience – sometimes even at the cost of our own health – that truly deep emotions affect our heart physically. Entering into the prayer of the heart is not possible unless we are determined to live very consciously and resolutely in contact with our corporal dimension. God created us so. Genesis tells us of Yahweh's creation of man from the mud of the earth, while at the same time asserting with total assurance that this material being is made in God's own image. Our body is not a hindrance to our relationship with God. On the contrary, it is the work of God himself who created us as his sons, called to receive him as their heritage.

The whole economy of the Incarnation of the Son of God places us within the same perspective. The early Church fought fiercely to defend the fact that Jesus really was man. He was born and lived in the flesh and in the flesh he taught us, suffered, died and was resurrected.

It is the human works of the Word of God which have given us, and continue to give us, life. God speaks to us in human words. Our sin is not purged in a symbolic manner but by the shedding of blood from the body of Jesus. He really died and was resurrected in the flesh. It is this material Resurrection which saves both our souls and our bodies. Indeed, the Holy Spirit was only given us as a fruit of the physical Resurrection of the Son. It is he, the son of Mary, who sends us the Holy Spirit from the bosom of the Father. It is not the uncreated Word but the Word incarnate who does so, after having shared our life and after becoming one of us.

We experience this incarnation each day through the sacraments, the liturgy, community life and our membership in the body of the Church. All these represent the tangible foundation, the presence in our lives, of the corporeal reality of Christ. Let us therefore welcome Jesus as he is, that is, as coming to us in our own bodily reality. Let us not hurry to be rid of this intermediary which we might be tempted to consider as an impurity in our relationship with God. This idea is wholly false: The body is not an impurity, but the very sanctuary in which we meet our Abba.

Even as it is impossible to consider community life as if our brothers were disembodied, pure spirits with whom our only contact would be outside and beyond their fleshly being, so would it be a refusal of the reality of the love of God to ignore the concrete physical reality of the Son who comes to us. The Eucharist which we celebrate each day is really the celebration of the Paschal act which resulted in fundamental changes in his body and his blood, not through abandoning or rising above them, but through giving them their full significance; they are a material reality which is the Son of God. In the same way, our body with all its unwieldiness, constraints and limitations is the reality which we are. It is my body which makes contact with that other reality of which Jesus said: 'This is my body.' It is the conjuncture of these two corporal realities which establishes the living connection between God and myself. 'Unless you eat the flesh of the Son of man and drink his blood, you have no life in you . . . As the living Father sent me, and I live because of the Father, so he who eats his bread will live forever' (John 6:55, 57).

The consequence of all this is that I cannot pray unless I pray from within my body. I cannot prescind from my incarnate reality when I turn to God. It is not simply a matter of religious discipline if certain movements are prescribed, or if I am limited by material conditions when I turn towards God. This is in line with the unique reality: God loves me as I am, as he made me to be. Why should I try to be more spiritual than he?

Hence, I learn to live on the level of my body, and within all the constraints which this places on me. Food, sleep, relaxation, illness, the limits of my strength – none of these constitutes an obstacle between God and myself. On the contrary, they are as a length of faultlessly woven cloth which swathes my concrete daily existence in the intimacy of divine reality.

Who among us has not had the experience, sometimes so terribly painful, of being hemmed in – almost imprisoned – by problems of health, for example? If our hearts be honest, we can only say one thing: it is God who comes to us in such grievous afflictions. In fact, they constitute the point at which the love of God enters into our life. Our heart welcomes God to the extent that it is attentive to this reality, which we might tend to consider inferior to our spiritual vocation. We must beware of this untruth which the Prince of lies seeks to instil in our heart. Let us not pretend to be pure spirits; we can be something better – children of God.

THE SPIRIT HIMSELF PRAYS WITHIN ME

We speak of praying, but do we know how to pray? Do I even know what constitutes real prayer? In all honesty, I have to admit that I do not know. Interiorly I feel a deep calling in this direction, but I remain in the dark.

Fortunately, 'The Spirit helps us in our weakness; for we do not know how to pray as we ought, but the Spirit himself intercedes for us with sighs too deep for words. And he who searches the hearts of men knows what is the mind of the Spirit, because the Spirit intercedes for the saints according to the will of God' (Romans 8:26–27).

Prayer lies in my heart. It springs from my heart. Yet, it is not something which I have created myself. It has been given to me by the Holy Spirit, who has penetrated my heart and who prays from within me. The Holy Spirit proceeds from the heart of God, with a longing to kindle in my own heart that same flame which burns in his.

We know all the passages in which St Paul stresses this, but do we not have a tendency to think of these in a purely theoretical way, or more nobly, as being realities of faith, that is, matters of which we speak with conviction but which in practice remain obscure? This presence of the Spirit in my heart would really exist only in God and be attained exclusively through intellectual formulas. The reality itself would totally escape my experience. But is that what St Paul meant?

While contending against all that is excessive in such an attitude, is it, on the other hand, necessary to insist that all genuinely Christian life is an experience of the Holy Spirit, similar to that of the Apostles' receiving tongues of fire on the morning of Pentecost? That has never been the teaching of the Church. However, between these two extremes, a genuine stance exists that is accessible to all Christians, whereby the presence in our lives of the Holy Spirit is a reality which has a direct influence over our way of being, our loving relationships with our brothers and sisters, and our prayer.

If we review the various stages we have discussed, we noticed a progression: renunciation of the idea that the centre of activity in prayer lies in our head and in speculative theories; opening the door into our own heart and discovering there a disorganized world of emotions and open wounds which emanate from our heart and which need to be purified. We then learned that there exists the possibility of effectively integrating all these open wounds of our heart into a redemptive process by bringing them into the open and offering them in all sincerity to the healing action of Jesus.

Thus, without actually pointing it out, we came to speak of the activity of the Holy Spirit within us. If we are able to put into practice the programme I have outlined, it means that the Spirit of the Lord is at work in us, allowing us to unravel from within the complex network of our emotions – something which, through patience and perseverance, we can offer to the purifying and resurrecting grace of the Saviour. Everything we have been discussing is already the work of the Spirit.

Let us continue along the same line. Besides noticing these disordered movements of the heart, especially after Jesus begins re-establishing his order within us, we also notice movements which are less disturbed and which even end up quite harmonious. Thus, without our being aware of it, the centre of our heart learns to reach out spontaneously towards our Lord. It is only after the event, and looking back at what has occurred, that we actually realize that our Lord's Spirit has been discreetly and silently at work in the depths of our heart. Gradually, as peace is established in these depths, a certain *mysterious dynamism* is set in motion with which we must learn to co-operate.

So we learn to integrate all the movements of our heart: the good, the not so good and even the bad, in order to be able to turn them towards God. Some of these movements come straight from God and return to him, while others need to be converted and transformed through the death and Resurrection of Jesus. All need to be consciously integrated into that dynamism of the Spirit spread throughout our hearts. It is a question of being alert to the movements of our heart, so that we can unite them freely and consciously to the work of the Holy Spirit within us.

None of this implies any mystical grace. It means being aware, with simplicity and gentleness, that our heart is alive and that we can offer this life to the Holy Spirit, to be carried in his own movement towards the Father.

St Paul states that the Holy Spirit intercedes for us with 'sighs

too deep for words'. This last phrase is noteworthy. The Holy
Spirit's normal activity is not to give us lucid ideas or special
lights, nor indeed, to give us anything in particular. The work
of the Holy Spirit is to draw us towards the Father. 'For all
who are led by the Spirit of God are sons of God. For you did
not receive the spirit of slavery to fall back into fear, but you
have received the spirit of sonship. When we cry, 'Abba!
Father!' it is the Spirit himself bearing witness with our spirit
that we are children of God' (Romans 8:14–15). The Holy
Spirit is a witness, a dynamic force which carries us forward.
We certainly do not seek to capture it, to plumb its nature or
control it. To attempt to do so would be to drive it out of our
hearts and to extinguish it. Let us leave the Spirit free to pray
within us in his own shrouded way, hidden and mysterious; we
will discern his action by its fruits. To the extent that we become
aware that we are learning how to pray, and, without knowing
exactly how we are able to make requests to God and have
them granted, to that extent we understand that the Holy Spirit
is praying within us, despite all our weaknesses.

and because

MY WEAKNESS: WHERE I DISCOVER AND
ENCOUNTER THE TENDERNESS OF THE FATHER

Let us return to some of the cardinal points which we have
discussed. Let us review them and integrate them, because they
represent the keystone of the prayer of the heart.

Fear of one's weaknesses is a basic reaction of any human
being. From the day we first realize, in one respect or another,
that we cannot rely on our own strength, a tendency to worry
takes root which can grow into great anxiety. All that we have
said up to now leads to the loss of personal security by bringing
to light what we have termed our vulnerability, our hidden
disorders and the limits of our created condition. Each time,
then, we have said to ourselves there is only one solution – to
recognize the reality of what we are and place it in the hands
of the Lord.

Recall the episode of the stilling of the waters. The Apostles
are panic-stricken by the way their boat is being tossed about

New way of saying Humility / how to achieve real communion

in the storm and go to wake Jesus. Astonished, he turns to them and asks: 'Why are you afraid, O men of little faith?' (Matthew 8:26). Then, with one gesture, he calms the waves.

So why be afraid of my own weaknesses? It is a fact that they exist; but for a long time I have refused to look them in the face. Gradually, I have assumed them, and am now obliged to recognize them as part of me. These are not extraneous to me, which I could rid myself of once and for all. Moreover, if I wished to forget them, the Father would soon bring them back to my attention. He would permit some fault or other in the face of which I would be unable to deny that I am a sinner. He would allow my health to play tricks on me, so that I would admit defeat and deliver myself defenceless to the love of the Father. He would make me realize, beyond the shadow of a doubt, how limited my abilities are.

What is new is that in the future these weaknesses, instead of representing a danger, give me the opportunity to make contact with God. For this reason I must gradually allow myself to become at ease with them, no longer considering them as a disturbing side of my personality, but as something willed and accepted by the Father; not as some hopeless inevitability but as a basic presupposition for the gift to me of divine life. When I suddenly find myself faced with a previously unknown weakness, my first reflex in the future will not be to panic but to ask myself where the Father may be hidden in it.

We cannot avoid asking ourselves a question: is this transformation of a weakness which seems to be nothing but defeat into a victory of love a sort of second thought on God's part, an alchemy whereby he changes evil into good or, on the contrary, are we not in the presence of a fundamental dimension of the divine order?

One could say a great deal about this. Let us be satisfied with simply stating that, even in the natural order, all true love is a victory of weakness. Love does not consist in dominating, possessing or imposing one's will on someone. Rather love is to welcome without defences the other as he or she comes to meet me. In return, one is sure of being welcomed unreservedly by the other without being judged or condemned, and without invidious comparisons. There are no contests of strength between two people who love each other. There is a kind of mutual understanding from within which a reciprocal trust emerges.

Such an experience, even if inevitably imperfect, is already a very compelling one. Yet it is but a reflection of a divine reality. Once we really begin to believe in the infinite tenderness of the Father, we are, as it were, obliged to descend ever more fully and joyfully into a realm in which we neither possess nor understand nor control anything.

Thus, almost without being aware of it, we enter into communion with the divine life. The relation between Father and Son in the Spirit is, at a level completely beyond our comprehension, a perfect embodiment of weakness transformed into communion.

In a way closer to ourselves, this intimate tenderness of the thrice-holy God is revealed in the relationship between the incarnate Son and his Father. We cannot help but be struck by the serenity and sense of infinite security with which Jesus quietly proclaims that he has nothing of his own, and that he can do nothing but what he sees the Father doing. What man would accept such powerlessness? Nevertheless, this is the path we must follow if we wish to live in the depths of our heart as God has made it, and as he transfigures it through the death and Resurrection of his Son.

Mary points us in the same direction. The Magnificat is at once a song of triumph and a recognition of total powerlessness. The two go hand in hand. From the beginning, she realized and accepted her utter weakness; thus does she find herself in a state of readiness to receive the Son which the Father gives her. She becomes the Mother of God because she is the closest to the poverty of God.

ENTERING INTO SILENCE

In following this path, it is normal that intellectual activity be gradually stilled during prayer; similarly, to the extent that the emotions of the heart are channelled, all kinds of distractions and diversions lose their sense. This means that, with an almost spontaneous movement, prayer of the heart leads us towards silence. Sometimes this experience is especially strong and inevitably one finds oneself exposed to what I might call the temptation of silence itself. Silence is a blessing which tends to seduce all hearts, once they have really had a taste of it. Yet there are many types of silence, not all of which are good. Indeed most types are distortions, rather than authentic prayer of the heart.

The first temptation is to make of silence an activity, even if we are entirely convinced we are doing the opposite. Basing ourselves on the fact that intellectual activity has ceased and that our heart is at rest, we imagine that we have achieved a genuine silence of all our being. In fact, even if it has a real value, this silence is the result of a tension on the part of the will which is the most subtle, but equally the most pernicious, of activities. Instead of keeping our heart attentive and alert, we maintain ourselves in an artificial state in which we are not receptive to the Lord but are relying on our own resources. In the case of people with strong and active wills, this can prove a major obstacle to attaining a state of readiness and openness to receive the Lord. Materially speaking, this silence is impressive, but it is a silence turned in on itself and dependent upon itself.

Another temptation is to make silence an end in itself. One imagines that the goal of prayer of the heart, and even of all contemplative life, is silence. One focuses on a purely material reality, rather than on the person of the Father, the Son or the Spirit. My inner state is what matters and not the relationship of loving receptivity which I have with God. I am no longer even praying; I am merely contemplating myself!

A similar temptation consists in making silence a reality in itself. Silence is everything! Once all the 'noise' of the senses, the mind and the imagination has been stilled, a genuine feeling of joy arises, and that is enough for us. We seek nothing more. We refuse to look for anything else. Any thought which might enter our minds even if it related to the Lord or came directly from him, would seem to us an obstacle. At such a time, the only divine reality is silence. There is no more prayer. There is nothing left but the casting of an idol called Silence.

It cannot be denied that authentic silence is very important and much to be prized. Nevertheless, if I wish to enter into genuine silence, it is essential to renounce silence from the bottom of my heart. I need not belittle or underestimate it, nor cease seeking it, but I must avoid making it a goal in itself.

Above all I must avoid believing that real silence is the result of my own efforts. I do not have to make silence from scratch, as though I were manufacturing something. Too often one thinks that silence only entails establishing peace in one's intellect, imagination and senses. This is one aspect of silence, but there is more to silence than that. It is also necessary that the very depths of the heart, to the extent that they reflect and express the will, should themselves be silent; that all desires be stilled other than that of doing the will of the Father. Instead of tensely imposing itself on the rest of my being, my will should abide in a state of pure receptivity, listening and welcoming. Only then does the possibility arise of entering into an authentic silence of all my being before God, a silence born of the genuine conformity of my deepest being with the Father, since it is created in his image and likeness.

God alone suffices; everything else is nothing. Genuine silence is the manifestation of this basic reality of all prayer. Silence truly exists in the heart once all the impurities which were opposed to the reign of the Father have disappeared.

True silence is only found in a pure heart, a heart that resembles the heart of God.

This is why a really pure heart is able to maintain complete silence, even when it is immersed in all sorts of activity, because there is no longer any discord between it and God. Even if its

intelligence and feeling remain active, in conformity with the
will of God, true silence continues to reign in such a heart.
'Blessed are the pure in heart, for they shall see God.'

12

A Devouring Fire

The Word of God will not endure falsehood. The Word is the breaking of the light of God into our little world. The proximity of God is not always comfortable. It is a fire which purifies, a hammer which shatters the hardness of our armour, a warrior who hurls himself on us, a sword which pierces our heart.

> 'Does not my word burn like fire
> – it is Yahweh who speaks –
> is it not like a hammer shattering a rock?'
> (Jeremiah 23:29 JB)

> Down from the heavens, from the royal throne,
> leapt your all-powerful Word, like a stern warrior . . .
> carrying your unambiguous command like a sharp
> sword . . .
> he touched the sky, yet trod the earth.
> (Wisdom 18:15)

The Word of God is something alive and active: it cuts like any double-edged sword but more finely: it can slip through the place where the soul is divided from the spirit, or the joints from the marrow; it can judge the secret emotions and thoughts. No created thing can hide from him; everything is uncovered and open to the eyes of the one to whom we must give account of ourselves. (Hebrews 4:12–13 JB)

Here is the surest means to become discerning (*hritihos*) of spirits and thoughts. If we open ourselves sincerely to the Word, it will separate the good from the bad in us, even to the most hidden depths of the soul. When in doubt, we should seek for light in the Word of God, whether in the Bible or from the lips

of a man led by the Spirit, who has assimilated the Word into
his life and gives us something of himself in conveying it to us.
The Word of God is unyielding. Sometimes because of weariness we would like to forget it, escape from it. Once it has
entered our heart, however, this is no longer possible. We may
fight against it, but in vain. As Jeremiah said:

> I used to say, 'I will not think about him,
> I will not speak his name any more.'
> Then there seemed to be a fire burning in my heart,
> imprisoned in my bones.
> The effort to restrain it wearied me,
> I could not bear it.
>
> (Jeremiah 20:9 JB)

AN IMPERISHABLE SEED

God sows the Word in our heart as a seed of life: 'Your new
birth was not from any mortal seed but from the everlasting
Word of the living and eternal God' (1 Peter 1:23 JB). It is
necessary to see clearly here. In the spiritual life it is not first
of all a matter of cultivating my virtues and my human intelligence, of developing the potentialities of my 'natural' life. There
is another life within, a life infinitely richer, and it is this life
that must be nurtured and liberated. My natural life is only the
raw material, the ground on which the seed is sown. Also,
the seed is received not only in the intelligence but in the depths
of the heart. It is the whole person, body and soul, who will be
transformed.

Through the sacraments of the faith I am reborn by water
and the Spirit into the life of Christ. God's life is rooted in the
depth of my heart as a treasure hidden in a field: a seed of life,
of knowledge and of love. My ascetic efforts are aimed at
ploughing and clearing the land so that the seed may grow
unobstructed. I remove the other plants and seeds in order that
all the energy in the soil may be available to nourish the one
essential seed, and there be absorbed and transformed into it.
The tilling of the soil, the preparation of the heart to welcome

the Word, has a number of moral and intellectual dimensions. The effort to initiate oneself into biblical languages and lore, the discipline that philosophy brings to the mind, systematic reflection in theology, all this is an asceticism of the mind which is useful and beneficial, according to each one's measure and grace. The danger would be to stay at the level of acquired knowledge and to treat the Word of God with a certain complacency, as a neutral object of study like any other, and thus lose the profound religious sense which ought to guide all our approaches to the Lord.

PREPARING THE HEART

The monk is always a beggar who asks humbly for a word of life. The most essential preparation of the heart is to acquire 'that eye whose clear gaze wounds the Spouse with love, the eye transparent and pure which sees God' (6.16). It is to the pure of heart that the vision of God is promised, and we aspire not only to speak more or less knowledgeably about God but to see him, to taste him, to cling to him. This may seem bold but that is how the Statutes define our vocation.

> Let Martha have her active ministry, very praiseworthy indeed, yet not without solicitude and agitation: nevertheless, let her bear with her sister, as she follows in the steps of Christ, in stillness knows that he is God, purifies her spirit, prays in the depths of her soul, seeks to hear what God may speak within her; and thus, tastes and sees – in the slender measure possible, though but faintly in a dark mirror – how good the Lord is; and also pours forth prayer for Martha herself. (3:9)

We are not invited to be theologians but to be contemplatives and mystics. We should not be afraid to use this word. To contemplate, to see, to taste God, such is the mystical life. It is characterized by the interiority of a prayer that abides in the heart, where the Lord speaks not by an external word but from within.

Of course, there is no problem with the word 'theologian'

when understood in its original meaning, as in Evagrius for example: 'If you are a theologian you truly pray; If you truly pray you are a theologian.' Here the theologian is one who knows God not at the level of words, but by personal experience.

On the other hand, the theologian in the modern sense of the word (he who speaks about God and gives lectures to instruct others) may be distinguished from the contemplative, and more precisely from the Carthusian. The charisms are different.* The knowledge of God in both cases is born from receptivity to the Word of God. The charism of the theologian is the charism of communication: the Word is understood by the intelligence and is communicated through human speech to others in a way that is comprehensible to them. This is the charism of the apostle.

LIKE MARY

The contemplative as such is a bit like Mary. He receives the Word as a lover's secret. He bears it in his heart as a seed of life from which Christ comes to birth little by little in a silent and, for him, obscure process, in obedience to a law of gestation which transcends and transforms him. The Word hollows out in him an abyss of silence and fills it with the poverty of the Spirit. The fruit is more of the order of life and love; very simple, it is hardly articulate at all. It is a matter of becoming rather than of speaking: 'And we, with our unveiled faces reflecting like mirrors the brightness of the Lord, all grow brighter and brighter as we are turned into the image that we reflect; this is the work of the Lord who is Spirit' (2 Corinthians 3:18 JB).

My face is unveiled, divested of its masks and defences and totally exposed to the light, but with confidence and without fear, while the Spirit in me cries out 'Father'. Our vocation is

---

*It is possible that both charisms may be found together in a particular theologian or monk, if this is in the interests of the Church. The issue is being considered here more abstractly.

indeed sublime: to be 'transfigured', changed in form, replaced by one who has no form, in being shaped to the image of Christ. Then I will reflect the face of Christ to the Father and to my brothers, a face of love and of truth.

I observe my features, as in a mirror, in the Spirit of God (James 1:23). The being hidden in the depths of the heart awakes, becomes conscious of the life within and stirs as a baby in its mother's womb. I leave a silent space in my heart for the Word of God to resound in all its purity. I silence my ideas, my narrow points of view and also my attempts to appropriate the Word of God to myself in too rational a way, thus restricting it to my own limited horizons in which I retain only what I can understand and what fits my categories. In prayer I prostrate before the Truth of God, I welcome the Word with humility into my heart, I let my spirit be shaped by it and remade in its image. 'Prayer is the key to divine mysteries' (Gregory Palamas).

III

Exodus in the Desert

13

Jesus in the Wilderness

**And Jesus, full of the Holy Spirit, returned
from the Jordan and was led by the Spirit
for forty days in the wilderness**
                                        (Luke 4:1–2)

Jesus has just been baptized. The Father has openly professed
his love for him and, filled with the Holy Spirit, he at once sets
out for the desert. This stay of our Lord in the wilderness is of
special significance for us. One of our General Chapters even
decided it would be useful to declare this officially in words
which have since been incorporated into the Statutes:

> The Lord and Savior of mankind deigned to live as the first
> exemplar of our Carthusian life, when He retired alone to
> the desert and gave Himself to prayer and the interior life:
> treating His body hard with fasting, vigils and other pen-
> ances; and conquering the devil and his temptations with
> spiritual arms. (2.10)

Bearing this in mind, and together with you, I would like to
listen to what Christ in the desert has to tell us in order
to receive from him the grace of better fulfilling our vocation.
In particular, I would hope that this might help us to be more
united to Jesus as he is guided by the Spirit in solitude.

In the first place, I am struck by the extreme sobriety of the
evangelists when they tell us of what Jesus did during those
forty days. Their discretion seems heavy with consequences

as to the attitude we should adopt towards Christ in such circumstances. We may be tempted at times to fill up the apparent gaps in the Gospel with embroidery from our own imagination. It is easy to think up a thousand details or images, all very pious, to flesh out our meditation and help us draw nearer to our Lord. Perhaps such an attitude is not reprehensible, but does it not run the risk of evading the austerity of the Gospels by creating a picture of the Saviour to our own liking?

It seems to me more honest to accept the poverty of the forty days spent in the wilderness. Let us try to approach them in a spirit of humility, not so as to enrich our feelings or increase our store of images, but to accept the truth of the word of God as it is revealed to us by the Holy Spirit.

We are told almost nothing of what happened during Jesus' long retreat, as he was led by the Spirit of God. Yet, at the same time, we are told by that same Spirit: draw from this source the living water which you need to become faithful dwellers in the desert. We must not allow ourselves to be frightened by the spiritual desert to which the Holy Spirit thus calls us, for a desert is indeed what it is. Going into the desert is not simply a matter of giving up frequent human contact; it also means adopting an attitude in which the inner dialogue is less and less concerned with new and attractive ideas but rather tends to concentrate on one person. Our abiding in the desert is justified for only one reason: we are there for Jesus.

Many of us realize that we have a natural attraction for solitude and aptitudes for a life with little human contact, drawn as we are by silence and a certain restfulness of our entire being. These natural attributes are very real; we need not disown them, and, in certain cases, there might even be the possibility of developing them in such a way that a sufficiently stable and harmonious solitary life could be built on them alone. But such a balance would know nothing of Jesus and would give rise to the suspicion that these words of our Lord might apply: 'He who is not with me is against me' (Matthew 12:30).

To enter truly into the desert to which God calls us, we have an initial decision to make: to build everything on the Son of God who came to receive everything from his Father in the solitude of the Judaean wilderness. All our natural tendencies must be sanctified and divinized by him so that our solitude becomes simply an entry into the heart of the eternally silent dialogue between Father and Son.

I wish to stress this wordless attraction which Jesus exerts on us. The Gospels, especially St John, reveal how seldom our Lord replies to questions or objections with proofs or demonstrations. Most of the time he just says: 'Believe in me. If you let yourself be led and enlightened by the Father, you will come to me and have eternal life.' Jesus is the source of life in the desert, not on account of his teachings, but because by his very nature he is a pole star and a centre of gravity for those whom the Father has interiorly called to follow and hearken to him.

Such then is the spiritual desert of which I spoke. The very depths of our heart, enfolded in solitude, are made, according to Hosea, to be allured by a secret call which can never be put into words. To travel through the desert means to walk in silence behind the guide. It is to follow Jesus.

The text from the General Chapter which I quoted, and Guigo in his Customs, tell us that Jesus in his solitude is an example for us. We must understand what this means, however. Does it indicate that our Lord, being in no need of solitude, deliberately entered it simply to give us the desire to imitate him? It would be intolerable, it seems to me, to suggest that Jesus, in order to teach us, should indulge in such play-acting.

Jesus is no comedian faithfully playing the role given him by the Holy Spirit. If he went into the wilderness, driven by the Spirit, it was because such a moment in the life of the Word incarnate was necessary to bring us back to the Father. According to the Gospel, Jesus in his humanity was capable of growing in wisdom and grace before God and man. He therefore had something to learn from his lone retreat in the desert, no doubt something fundamental and of great importance; for it is the first stage in his journey after the Father had proclaimed him the object of his special favour. The temptations undoubtedly reveal the very real trials which the Messiah had to undergo in order to assume the full weight of humanity – both his and ours – in his call to accomplish its salvation. The heart which was subjected for forty days to the poverty of spirit to which I have referred was reduced to its fundamental condition: that of having to make an explicit choice, either to place complete and infinite trust in God, or to take up a stance against God as Satan did. One cannot help but recall the two analogous temptations which were the starting points for our ancestors in the flesh and in the spirit: Adam and Abraham. The first was faced with the wiles of the serpent, the second called by God to sacrifice his only son, the sole bearer of the covenant promises. Each found himself in a situation in which he had to surpass the accessory, the futile and the transient, and denude himself of all but the essential: the ability to dialogue with God and the liberty to say yes or no to him.

This is the real vocation of every man who has attained the use of his reason. Yet we know how everyday experience brings worries, distractions and instability in its train like a fog, and makes it hard for us to see clearly the choice which lies before us. Few men preoccupied with worldly affairs have the strength to enter fully into their interior desert to face up to temptation, the basic test of their dignity as creatures made in the image of God. Every man needs help to enter his personal desert and confront what he finds there.

During his forty days in the desert, Jesus sanctified it by the use he made of it, and transformed it into a place of freedom in which his followers can choose God, as he did, from the depths of their heart. Through silence, fasting and temptation, Jesus became fully himself, able to place his whole trust in the Father. Following his example, we must also become our true selves in the desert, ridding ourselves of every impediment in order that we may give ourselves to God joyfully and become his children. May it please God that we, in our turn, become as Christ, wellsprings of interior freedom for those who, deprived of the grace of the desert, have difficulty becoming themselves.

I would like to add a few more words about what appears to me an essential element of Jesus' sojourn in the wilderness as stressed by the evangelists: the presence of the Holy Spirit. It was the Spirit who took possession of him after his Baptism;

it was the Spirit who led him into the desert and was his guide during forty days; he left the wilderness imbued with the power of the Spirit. Hardly back in Galilee, in the synagogue of Nazareth, his first words are a commentary on the prophecy of Isaiah: 'The Spirit of the Lord is upon me' (Luke 4:18).

Here again I would not wish to paraphrase the word of God, but I am struck by the intimate compenetration between Jesus and the Spirit. How can we possibly call ourselves disciples of Jesus in the desert unless we, too, deliver ourselves completely into the hands of the Spirit and try to respond to his every inspiration? Yet what does that mean? Never has monastic tradition referred to a special gift of the Spirit reserved to monks in the desert.

At the same time, I cannot help making a connection between this complete self-giving to the Spirit and two of our fundamental texts on obedience. The first is that of Bruno to his beloved Converse Brothers of Chartreuse. Their obedience seems to him exemplary, and was a sign to him that they lived as true contemplatives, wholly given over to God's action or, in other words, to his Spirit.

The second text is Guigo's declaration to the newly professed in his Customs. What he says is so basic that it has been retained in every edition of our Statutes:

> For as all who wish to live according to a rule must observe obedience with great zeal, we, in the measure that the way of life we have embraced is more exacting and austere, must observe it the more ardently and carefully; lest, if – which God avert – obedience is lacking, such great labors may well go unrewarded. (10.11; 18.13)

That is to say, our life in the desert pleases God only if it is lived in an attitude of complete receptivity, through obedience.

Our first Fathers certainly did not perceive obedience primarily in juridical terms, but as a canal, so to speak, of the Spirit. To live in obedience is to leave oneself open to the breath of God; it is the most direct route to learning how to live permanently under the guidance of the Spirit. Whatever the strictures of Bruno or Guigo, we can never seek to evade them if we truly wish to follow Jesus, filled with the Holy Spirit, into the desert.

Perfect harmony exists between the two: obedience and the Spirit.

These thoughts on Jesus in the desert are austere. Nonetheless we should not see in them any justification for living in our desert in a mean and stunted way, bereft of impetus and enthusiasm. On the contrary, it is with joy that we should welcome this message. We are called to live night and day in dependence on the Spirit as true sons of God. We are invited to cry out to him: 'Abba! Father!' (Romans 8:15). Amen.

14

The Threefold Temptation

We bear within us at one and the same time the power, purity and love of the Holy Spirit and the wounds and weaknesses deposited in our nature by sin. The harmony of truth and the unity of love develop in us only through a slow process of healing, through grace, the action of God in us but not without us; it demands our co-operation, a persevering ascesis that frees us from the anarchy of disordered passions and establishes in us the order of love, repose, *hesychia*. The Adversary still lurks around us, and he finds many complicities in us. We know that the final victory is assured to us in Christ, if we stand fast in faith, hope and love. 'In the world you face persecution. But take courage; I have conquered the world!' (John 16:33).

Jesus showed us the Way, the Truth and the Life. Let us look towards him. 'Christ suffered for you, leaving you an example, so that you should follow in his steps' (1 Peter 2:21).

> Let us also lay aside every burden and sin that clings so closely, and persevere in running the race that lies before us, while keeping our eyes fixed on Jesus, the leader and perfecter of faith. For the sake of the joy that lay before him, he endured the cross, despising its shame, and has taken his seat at the right hand of the throne of God. (Hebrews 12:1–2)

Ancient tradition saw a continuity between the testimony of the martyr's blood and the life of the monk, not only in the sense of a historical succession in time, the monk taking over from the martyr, but more profoundly in the total gift of love which is, or ought to be, the same in both cases.

The first monks went deep into the desert with the intention of recovering the unity of a heart fixed only on God and also to struggle hand to hand with the Adversary, where Christ confronted and conquered him for the spiritual welfare of the Church.

Jesus' response to Satan is the renunciation of every earthly reward, and perfect adherence to the Father's will for love of the Father alone; to live by every word of God, not to tempt God, to worship God alone and to serve only him.

It is the same paschal mystery that is realized in us. Let us try to see, or to foresee, the concrete form that this can take for us.

THE FIRST TEMPTATION: THE TEST OF FAITH

'He humbled you by letting you hunger' (Deuteronomy 8:3). If we have entered into the desert, it was in response to the word of God. The Lord called us by a hidden name which we recognized as our true name, our true desire. He addressed our liberty, and we responded by our faith. 'Follow me,' he said, and we gave up all we possessed to follow in his steps the way of spiritual liberty, in poverty, chastity and obedience. That dispossession of ourselves was realized by us on entering monastic life, as far as we were capable; our intentions, at least, were radical. But deep indeed were the roots of our attachment to earthly nourishment, to everything that nourishes our need for self-affirmation, self-love, autonomy, possession, human love, sensible gratification, etc. Sons in our Father's house, have we not the right to taste the perfectly good pleasures of his creation? After 'forty days' of fasting, we are hungry. God withdraws the sensible consolations of the first days and hides himself in the mystery of absence.

God was 'testing you to know what was in your heart' (Deuteronomy 8:2). Real hunger is called by its real name. We experience our elementary needs; we come to know ourselves as poor people depending on the produce of the earth and on others. As centres of strong passions, we are no angels. Nature claims its due with insistence. The manna of spiritual nourishment seems tasteless, illusory, distant. Our renunciation was a dream, a mistake, a mutilation of our human person, a masochistic suicide, a megalomaniac desire to be God . . . Christ died on the Cross, that is certain. The Resurrection, what do we know? The theologians themselves speak about it in an increasingly embarrassed and contradictory way. So, let us live our life as a man of this earth, on this earth.

'One does not live by bread alone, but by every word that comes from the mouth of God' (Matthew 4:4). One day, on awakening in the cold light of morning, we see our true face, the same face that we had before our conversion. What then of faith, Christ's call? Beyond an overheated imagination and the blindness of our sensibility, was there nothing? But no, there must have been something, for our poverty is not the same. It is more profound. It assumes the reality of our human needs, which we are; but it discovers deep down within us, beyond merit, virtue, reason, an abyss of poverty so deep that only God can fill it. This poverty is the face of our physical death glimpsed one day, and we accept dying. Yet, it is also our heart's unlimited capacity for life, for light and love, and we go to meet the death which we believe opens out onto eternal life, the only 'true' life. We anticipate it. We embrace the restrictions of our life, the renunciations that Christ demands and his Cross, with faith in Him who is the Way, the Truth and the Life. They open us to the freedom of a superior life of love. We bear witness to our faith before the world by abstaining from possessions which are real, but partial. We long for the Lord to come to fill our poor heart with his presence. Maranatha!

The hunger for earthly nourishment will remain, and in order to keep the desire for Life alive, we always have to recommence the work of dispossession. An energetic effort is necessary above all at the beginning of the spiritual life, but it must be sustained; only beginners who are a little weary are under the illusion that they are above all that. Yet our effort is only one dimension of the process that will reach the perfection of liberty when the Spirit enables the heart to nourish itself on the Word, substantially, from within (though, perhaps, aridly on the sensible level). Only the Spirit can enable us to serve God alone, without the support of any earthly reward, for God alone.

No earthly reward: neither recognition nor glory nor repute

in the eyes of men; neither sensible consolations (even spiritual), nor facility in virtue, nor light nor special gifts; no temporal profit from the gift of God's grace. The Church has not always been able to remain at those heights of spiritual detachment at every epoch, for it is composed of frail persons, of little faith at times. Nor do monks always have cause to boast. Yet every attempt to convert the spiritual communion God gives us into temporal goods has been a disaster. We monks, at least, and above all solitaries, ought to bear witness in our life to the absolute primacy of the spiritual. Our wealth is our poverty: that is the law of love.

'My food is to do the will of him who sent me and to complete his work' (John 4:34). The word of God does not set itself before us as an object of contemplation and nothing more. It expresses God's will in our regard; it challenges us; it requires our obedience. To do the will of God is Christ's food, his life, and it should be ours as well. That is the meaning of our vow of obedience: the desire to bring our will into line, in everything, with the will of God. That will is communicated to us, not only by the revealed Word, but also by the Church of Christ, whose most immediate representatives are our religious superiors. Obedience inserts us into the current of life of the Spirit from which the Church draws its life and incarnates that life in us. If we give up the fundamental good of human liberty, it is in order to enter into the liberty of God by conformity, as perfectly as possible, to his will. We know that the liberty of God does a work of love, a work of salvation for men, and it is at the heart of this obedience of love that we share in a most real way in Christ's work of redemption. With him, let us abandon ourselves to the Father's will; it was 'his work' on earth. Thus we enter obscurely into the essential life of the Son, in the bosom of the Trinity, as total gift to the Father in the Spirit. Obedience is a communion of love, for Christ, and also for us: 'For the love of God is this, that we obey his commandments' (1 John 5:3).

We know that this obedience was not easy for Jesus. Yet we understand that the intransigence shown during the temptation in the desert was necessary; for only a total renunciation of all self-seeking, a perfect selflessness, could face the destitution of the Cross, a poverty made absolute by the Father who, mysteriously, abandons his Son. It is obedience to the Father which brings Christ to that point. 'Not what I want, but what you want' (Mark 14:36).

We must follow Christ into that desert of the surrender of ourselves, beyond our comprehension and our limited horizons; surrender to a love so great as to transform us into itself, and make of us a perfect gift to the Father.

THE SECOND TEMPTATION: THE TEST OF HOPE

'Do not put the Lord your God to the test.' Walk with an unshakeable faith in the Word of God. As signs, the Father has given you the creation which reflects his beauty, and his interventions throughout the whole history of salvation, especially his ultimate manifestation in Christ and in the Church. The Father has said everything in his Son, and we await nothing more.

In the first days of the monastic life, heaven is very near, and the road that leads there seems short. As the years go by, the objects of our faith can become more remote and lose their consistency. In fact, our faith, more and more purified, touches them in a truer and deeper way, but our sensibility is unsatisfied and goes hungry. This is the test of duration, of perseverance in God's silence. We are tempted to demand a sign, some tangible sign of that love of God in which we believe, but which we do not see. It is difficult for us to trust solely in God's promises. The man of prayer, the solitary, sows in the night. He does not see any harvest, but holds out in faith. The Adversary will try to confuse the sensational into the supernatural, perhaps in the form of spectacular graces, of extraordinary states of soul, eccentricities which are provoked or allowed, etc.

Against these temptations, we must learn to rely on God alone, in pure faith, to expect everything from God alone in pure hope, and not demand any other assurance apart from his Word.

'Is the Lord in our midst or not?' In practice, this has far-reaching implications. The failure of our social insertion into

the monastery, even of our programme of sanctity as we conceived it, can give us the impression of being abandoned and
forgotten by God and of being failures. Moreover, this can be
a trial undergone by a monastery or an entire order. Despair
easily arises in solitude in the absence of any feedback.* We
lose our sense of identity in relation to others. It is the moment
to stake one's all on God, to hope against hope, to be reborn
in faith. Our hope is the power that carries the world towards
its plenitude in God, that is to say, towards Christ. The monk
is essentially a man of hope. That is the secret of many hidden,
humble and cheerful lives with nothing extraordinary on their
surface, just like Mary's.

THE THIRD TEMPTATION: THE TEST OF LOVE

'Worship the Lord and serve only him.' This time the test is
not through poverty but through riches. 'When you have eaten
your fill, take care that you do not forget the Lord, who brought
you out of the land of Egypt, out of the house of slavery'
(Deuteronomy 6:11–12). When he is satiated, man is in danger
of forgetting the Giver of every gift. Jesus, faced with the
example of the rich young man incapable of divesting himself
of his possessions, is categorical: 'Truly I tell you, it will be
hard for a rich person to enter the kingdom of heaven. Again I
tell you, it is easier for a camel to go through the eye of a needle
than for someone who is rich to enter the kingdom of God'
(Matthew 19:23–24).

A man is rich if he possesses something. In fact, we need
certain things: food, clothes, shelter, etc. Our vow of poverty
is intended to cure all excess in the possessive instinct. We
receive what we really need from the community. We do not

---

*By 'feedback', I mean the reflection of ourselves that others mirror back
to us by their words, attitudes, etc., towards us. It is partly in that mirror
that we see ourselves, and it thus determines our self-image. One aspect
of personal maturity, especially for the Carthusian, is sufficient autonomy
not to have an inordinate need of this feedback. We always have a certain
need of it, however, which, concretely, the community dimension of our
life ought to satisfy.

possess anything special for ourselves, to the exclusion of our brothers. Why set oneself against this natural inclination of ours, the most widespread motive for activity in our consumer society? Most people expend all their energy in an effort to have more and more. A person's standing is usually measured by what he has: his house, his car, etc., not by what he is. There precisely lies the danger. Man is alienated, possessed by what he possesses. 'The love of money is a root of all evil' (1 Timothy 6:10). The human person is made subordinate to objects. We become 'slaves to various passions and pleasures' (Titus 3:3). Ultimately, they become our gods. St Paul goes to the root of the problem when he speaks of that 'greed which is idolatry' (Colossians 3:5).

We are obliged to struggle against our innate propensity to compensate for a deep poverty on the level of being with riches on the level of having, whether it be material objects, learning, or even virtues (in so far as they are acquired habits).

Satan offers Christ 'all the kingdoms of the world and their splendour' (Matthew 4:8). That would be the political realization, on this earth, of the Kingdom of God, hence something apparently good. 'Apparently', for the price is to worship Satan and put him in the place of God. This happens when one takes human power and glory as the supreme value and norm. Such options are not absent from human history.

The Kingdom of Christ is not of this world. In our modest capacity, to try to wield power over our brothers (even in spiritual matters), to push ourselves forward unduly, to lose sight in the concrete of the primacy of spiritual means (prayer, love, poverty) in bringing to realization the Kingdom among men, all that is to yield to this temptation.

HERE THERE IS NO WAY

Yet, this temptation appears in a more subtle and interior form. Our journey towards God is a movement towards the invisible Father, towards him who dwells in unapproachable light (1 Timothy 6:16). The concepts of the faith reveal him to us, but never adequately; their final word is 'mystery'. Even Christ, perfect image of the Father, radiance of his glory (who sees him, sees the Father), manifests the Father as much as a created sacrament can do, but never violates the secret of the transcendence of God. Jesus remains the Way that leads to the Father: a Way to follow, a tension of love that passes ever beyond, towards him who is always beyond.

The deepest knowledge that spiritual men have of God lies in the experiences they have of him, of his action and of his presence in their heart and in their prayer. But if a man halts at one of these experiences, however lofty or true it may be, he ends up adoring an idol.

We must never install ourselves in anything whatever, except in God alone. Love requires it and spiritual poverty must go that far. Acts of the theological virtues of faith, hope and love reach God as he is in himself, and not just as partially refracted in the concepts of faith. Yet this is only true if one surrenders to their dynamism of love that plunges into the unknown depths of the Mystery and leaps up towards the One who remains hidden behind the wall. The life of prayer involves an endless transcending, a refusal to settle down, a thirst for the infinite, which shatter, one after the other, the pious and reassuring idols that we tirelessly construct, one after the other. That is the desert.

It is possible to live for years alone in a cell, occupied solely with the things of God, without even crossing the threshold of true solitude, for want of giving up an infantile world peopled with images, spiritual pleasures and endless discourses. It is a whole world which only reflects the multiple faces of our own ego and our unconscious desires. It is the ego that we are in danger of worshipping, rather than God. Images, sensibility, concepts, are things we need, but we must know how to go beyond them, to leave the husk behind in order to immerse ourselves in the silence of faith, in the humility of solitude, in the shoreless infinity of love.

Away with you, Satan! Our thoughts are not God's thoughts. The way of faith is a path which is not a path. It is the mysterious world of the Resurrection. It is Christ, his death and his life. It is the Spirit that blows where it wills. It is the Father whose infinite love cannot be inscribed within limits.

Let us allow ourselves to be borne away by the Spirit to the Father, with an ever-renewed surrender in Christ.

We know that the Son of God has come, and has given us understanding to know the One who is true; and we are in the One who is True, in his Son Jesus Christ. He is the true God and eternal life. Little children, be on your guard against idols. (1 John 5:20–21)

15

Isaac Regained

(Theme of Perseverance)

The story of the temptation of Abraham is not 'edifying' in the ordinary sense of the term (any more than is the Cross of Christ); it is awe-inspiring and creates disquiet. One could not lightly propose it as a model for everyone. Our Lord taught us rather to pray: 'Lead us not into temptation'. No one should rely on his own strength. Such a trial is bearable only if God takes the initiative and gives the strength to bear it. Who, in fact, knows for certain what he believes? And Isaac is only restored to him who does not doubt. That is where the real paradox of the story lies: that Isaac is regained. All too easily, we identify the courage of faith with the courage of renunciation. Certainly one cannot dispense with renunciation. Only he who has raised the knife receives Isaac. But the courage of faith goes further.

Faith begins with the total gift of oneself to God; that is absolutely necessary. But this God is a God who promises, and the eyes of faith are directed towards the fulfilment of the promise. Isaac is born. So faith finds, at the human level, a concrete fulfilment. This points from afar to the perfect fulfilment: the vast multitude of peoples yet to be born; but the first link of the chain is already given; faith possesses a human support.

(Letter to the Hebrews)

Now, because of his fidelity to this God in whom he believes, Abraham prepared to sacrifice Isaac who seemed, humanly speaking, the indispensable means to the fulfilment of the promise. Yet Abraham continues to hold fast in faith and hope to the Word of God in all its fullness; he goes on trusting in the promise God has never revoked. And so, at this moment, his faith has no longer any other support than that of blind trust in God, despite the impossibility – humanly evident – of seeing the promise fulfilled. It is then, and only then, that he regains the fruit of this promise, but with hands he knows to be wholly empty, as pure gift of God's grace, a gift utterly transparent to the love of the giver. From now on, the divine love is free to take possession of, and pour out the abundance of its riches upon, the man who has become wholly poor, pure receptivity; the man for his part will not claim the gift as his own, nor pride himself because of it. But note well: the positive orientation of faith, the thirst for life, love, being, which are the motivating forces behind it, were genuine and have found fulfilment, paradoxically but truly, and in a certain sense, already in this life. Isaac has been regained. It remains true, however, that something in Abraham's relationship with God and with his son will never again be as before.

Monastic life can sometimes present a certain similarity.* The beginner in the religious life renounces all to follow Christ. But he is like a man entering the desert for the first time. He cuts off the human supports of his life and rejects the precious waters of freedom, human love, etc. This he does with great generosity, but with a courage sustained by the presumption born of inexperience. Lofty ideals seem within his reach and he sees himself surrounded with a sort of aura of glory. Little by little, the gift of himself in faith takes root in the monastic life. It is structured by it and takes a visible form, which is at the same time its expression and support. That is absolutely essential if the delicate seed of his vocation is to grow. His mind is elated by the light he derives from the contemplation of divine revelation; his will is strengthened by the order and harmony of a life where each step has meaning; his senses delight in the austere beauty of the chant; his heart is cheered by the presence of brethren walking alongside him on the same road. He has written his promise on a document; that promise

---

*We are describing a kind of experience of the religious life in relation to our subject although aware that there are others equally valid and more simple. But it is a kind of experience by no means rare in our troubled days; the outcome is not always happy.

has been accepted by the Church. The Kingdom of God is already beginning to be realized, visibly.

All that is good; it is the fruit of his faith, his prayer, the fulfilment of the promise, the divine blessing, it is 'Isaac'. He has to use the human resources that God provides for him; to neglect to do so would often be the presumption that 'tempts God'. But the sort of security these means afford him, the light and warmth they bring, could also turn them into screens against a light and warmth infinitely more subtle, beyond man's grasp; against a lack of support infinitely stronger than the little righteousness according to man's measure that he painstakingly seeks to build, and behind which he runs the risk of settling down, sheltered against the far more exacting demands of this God who knows no measure. One is so at home among things, ideas, rules and ceremonies; there, one is master! One pays the tithe of adoration to God, but one takes good care that the doors which might allow God himself to enter are kept securely closed.

But the years go by, and before the monk's eyes the horizon constantly recedes. He learns the value of the water he once relinquished so lightheartedly, through the agonizing effects of thirst. Powerless, he sees his body growing weaker, and his force failing as weariness sets in. He seems to be forgetting where he is going and why. What good is a heart so dried up as to seem incapable of loving others, and so God himself? For we have but one heart with which to love. Are the means perhaps destroying the end? Gradually – or in a sudden crisis – the meaning of his life will be put in question.*

Perhaps he will stumble upon a source of earthly water, pure and fresh, in some hidden oasis. A very considerable moral

---

*It is a well-known fact that one of the great turning points in a man's life, when the orientation of his life tends to be radically questioned, comes towards the years of maturity. At that time of life in particular, the religious often achieves the fundamental ratification of his vocation or, on the other hand, chooses another way. The true motives of such decisions are known only to God (in actual fact a mistake may have been made at the beginning, or perhaps the way irrevocably lost in the course of the journey); we should not pass judgement on anyone lest we ourselves be tempted beyond our forces.

effort is then called for, if he is to refrain from satisfying this thirst which is at the root of his soul – an effort incomparably greater and more painful than his initial renunciation.

By now the monk is humble and free from illusion. The sand of life which he holds in his hand is flowing rapidly through his fingers; he has difficulty in seeing beyond the limits of human horizons; he knows his poverty, his human frailty, his human heart. He is unsure if he still really believes in what he is unable to see. Ritual and ceremonial have little to say to him; the repetition of acts, to which no interior spontaneity corresponds, tends to produce a certain alienation of his personality. The well-organized structures of his life hedge him in like prison bars where all seems sterile and dead. His contact with his brethren is purely external, as that of a passer-by; he feels isolated, a stranger.

This means that God is taking Isaac back and the monk must surrender freely what appears from a human point of view to be the indispensable means of the realization of the promise, of the Kingdom of God – that which seemed to be the Kingdom – and this he must do without hesitation, without abandoning the quest of the Absolute, of the love that now seems to be falling to pieces and an illusion. He must hold fast in faith and hope to the Word of God and the promise of Christ, to the power of the Spirit of Christ to give life to what appears to be dead, with no other support for faith save that of 'blind' trust in God alone. That is the courage proper to faith: the courage to believe that one receives – and to receive in fact already – all, absolutely all, from the sheer bounty of God's love.

The situation is no longer the same as at the beginning. It is not now a question of choice between different lifestyles, all equally full of promise, which present themselves to the beginner. Life is a one-way road: there is no possibility of turning back. The man who has been put to the test harbours no illusion as to the possibility of complete self-fulfilment, the satisfaction of his heart's deepest yearnings, at a purely human level. He knows he is made for God; he is too marked now. The choice offered to him is one between a life which has transcendent meaning (though perceived only in the obscurity of faith) and one where this meaning would, in fact, be accorded a secondary place, very far away, so as to rest content with a water within our reach and capacity. But one should not deceive oneself as to the real possibility of such a choice: how many among the people of our time choose the waiting in darkness? When you are genuinely longing for a drink, a cup of water is extremely attractive. That's how we are . . .

Once again one has to leave everything in the Lord's hands, but an 'everything' more justly estimated and more deeply loved; not with bitterness and despair, but in the confidence of faith that in Christ we possess everything – even for the present.* This offering must be genuine, it must be total. If it is, it may well be that 'Isaac' will be given us† in God, even in this life; but it will be a gift consecrated to God by the sacrificial act, under the sign of Christ, and in a way *within Christ*: an 'Isaac' who, in Christ, is pure joy, yet who one knows will be fully given only in the fullness of Christ, and then for all eternity; an 'Isaac' possessed in hope.

The monk, the Christian, is necessarily a man of hope whose whole being reaches out in faith towards the true water of life and eternal love, and who, throughout his whole journey, is sustained by this water, as from an inner and hidden source.

Come, Lord Jesus!

Means Laughter. our Isaac is Jesus

God is love

Out of mind to bottom of heart

down into the soul Hold onto the eternal soul

We do possess. God & Richness – We are Children of God

*'Manifold more *in this time* and in the age to come eternal life' (Luke 18:29–30).

†Consolation, brotherhood, the positive meaning of the institution, all could be regained, but it is perhaps in the sphere of personal relationships, from now on 'in Christ', that the greatest deepening is possible.

Your heart lives on what you love (Holy Spirit) – heart belongs here.

16

The Dangers that Lurk

At times, the divine manna seems insipid to us and we are homesick for the 'onions of Egypt', for the pleasures and feelings more within the reach of the carnal man that we are. That is normal. Our life is simple; its joys are natural; the spiritual gives itself under the veil of faith. And we are agitated, dispersed, complicated, tormented by all kinds of desires and obscure impulses. One has to work for a long time before everything is integrated and harmonized. Let us know how to react. Let us have a sense of our responsibility before the Church. Let us try to live out always, or more and more and on the level of faith, our co-operation in Christ's work. Let us forsake ourselves, and stop worrying about our own tiny personality (the solitary, for example, becomes a hypochondriac very easily: a pain will always be found somewhere!) in order to lose ourselves in the vast expanses of Christ, of love, love for ourselves and for our brothers. The secret is never to separate oneself from Christ, the Life, the Way, the Truth. The enemy is our self-love, our ego.

> He knocked at the beloved's door and a voice asked from within, 'Who is there?' He answered, 'It is I.' And the voice said, 'This house would not hold both you and me.' And the door remained closed. Then the lover withdrew into the forest and prayed and fasted in solitude. One year later he journeyed back and knocked again at the door, and again the voice asked, 'Who is there?' And the lover replied, 'It is you.' Then the door opened to let him through. (A Sufi poet, Jalal al-Din al-Rumi)

It is true and beautiful, is it not? Now let us listen to the

Word of God in the Book of Revelation. Let us note the depth
to which God descends, his humility. Here, it is Christ who
stands at the door of our heart and knocks, like a beggar. But
the space is already taken.

> 'For you say, "I am rich, I have prospered, and I need
> nothing." You do not realize that you are wretched, pitiable,
> poor, blind and naked. Therefore I counsel you to buy from
> me gold refined by fire so that you may be rich, and white
> robes to clothe you and to keep the shame of your nakedness
> from being seen; and salve to anoint your eyes so that you
> may see . . . Listen! I am standing at the door, knocking; if
> you hear my voice and open the door, I will come in to you
> and eat with you, and you with me.' (Revelation 3:17–20
> NRSV)

We should not have too idealized a notion of solitude. The
desert is ambivalent, like our hearts. A place of communion
with God, it is also a place of trial, of dryness, of sterility.

Guigo told us its advantages; experience often reveals its
drawbacks. Let us listen to an eminent Carthusian of the last
century, Dom François de Sales Pollien:

> Solitude! We have come in search of it. Those who seek it
> are few, and of those who find it, do they all derive benefit
> from it? Solitude, in principle, is a powerful means of elev-
> ation; in practice, it is at times a terrible means of
> depression. Solitude is the principal stumbling block of
> vocations that fail and the principal difficulty in vocations
> that persevere. Solitude is the great question mark when we
> enter, and the somber enigma throughout our Carthusian
> life. Solitude always ends in ecstasy: that from on high or
> that from below. Man emerges from it an angel or a beast
> says St Bernard. (Chapter Sermon)

The Statutes are no less realistic:

> How, then, can we fulfil our role in the People of God of
> being living sacrifices acceptable to God, if we allow relax-
> ation and immortification of life, distraction of mind and
> useless conversation, vain cares and trivial occupations to

separate us from the Son of God – from Him who is life itself and the Supreme Sacrifice? Or if a monk in cell is held captive by a miserable anxiety arising from love of self? In simplicity of heart, then, and in purity of mind let us strive with all our power to fix our thoughts and affections continually on God. Let each be forgetful of self and what lies behind, and press on towards the goal to win the prize which is God's call to the life above, in Christ Jesus. (33.3)

17

In Spirit and in Truth

We are all like the Samaritan woman in the Gospel. The Lord offers us true life, the gift of the Spirit, which will become in us 'a spring welling up to eternal life'. We are happy to receive this sublime gift, but we have great difficulty in remaining at that height. We trivialize it, we degrade it, we reduce it to our measure, an object to possess among others, merits to accumulate, an insurance against death, a fetish against the fear of life, an excuse for our incapacity to love. We surround it with all kinds of defences like a fragile plant: ritual and moral prohibitions, exclusions of every sort.

But that is not the living water that Christ gives. On the contrary, his is a dynamic force of love, the Spirit of love (John 7:39), which shatters all limits and all divisions (4:21). It matters little whether we worship on the mountain of Samaria or on that of Jerusalem, provided it is done in spirit and in truth, that is, in the love poured into our hearts by the Holy Spirit, and in the truth brought to us by Christ. St Paul says: 'Where the Spirit of the Lord is, there is freedom' (2 Corinthians 3:17). And St John repeats untiringly that it is by the love we have for God and for our neighbour that 'we know that we are living in God and he is living in us, because he lets us share his Spirit' (1 John 4:12-13).

The gift we have received is a flowing spring that carries us (we do not carry it!), that vivifies us and makes us capable of loving in truth, in Christ; it is the source of adoration of the Father. Meditate on that extraordinary phrase: 'The Father seeks' these worshippers. The Father seeks us, because we wish to adore him in truth, and we seek the Father. That is the drama of our life. And it is possible that it is to the indifferent and unworthy sinner in us that the Lord, oblivious of protocol, will offer his living water. There is a continuity between the water of the well and eternal water. Love, to the extent that it is true, is always identical to itself, always eternal. It is traditional to apply the image of living water to the grace of contemplation (see, for example, St Teresa of Jesus) and the effort to draw water from the well to meditation. That falls within the perspective of our programme of deepening our life of prayer, without separating it from a deepening of the life of Christ in us, and of the ascendance of the Spirit over our heart. The result should be the welling up in us of that adoration which is one of the highest fruits of love, of the Spirit in us, and which can only lead us to the truth of a silence full of praise, and of a solitude charged with communion. But I am afraid of being caught in the snare of words here. 'To adore in spirit and in truth.' We all desire it – or at least, we think we desire it. For the truth will burn us, just as the Spirit eludes our control and leads us where we do not wish to go.

It was so simple at the beginning! To adore meant expressing a homage full of respect, veneration and obedience through ponderous chants, solemn prayers, hieratic gestures, a moral conduct governed by well-established rules, silent interior prayer and finally by a love full of gratitude. We were not bad; we were sure of this God of ours and a little self-satisfied.

So, one after another, the elements of this solidly constructed world collapse. They all depended on a certain idea of God, and this idea has vanished. One spoke a great deal of the death of God a few years ago, often in an unacceptable way. But you will permit me the risk of saying that for all of us God must die at a certain moment. In one sense, only the atheist (a-theos, without-God) can truly believe in God. Let me explain: it is necessary that the God of our imagination die, the God of our projections and desires (who is none other than our Ego deified); the God who stands alongside the cosmos as some-'thing' else, who stands alongside the neighbour as someone else, in competition with him or her to win my love, the God of whom it suffices to know the general moral rules in order to do his will; the God infinitely above his creatures' pains in a transcendence beyond reach; the God-judge, who punishes in accord with a justice conceived along human lines; the God who blocks the spontaneity of life and love. Such a God must die to make room for a God strangely close and familiar and nevertheless totally beyond our grasp; a God who bears a human face – that of Christ, that of my brother; who is love in a way that defies all our human notions of justice; who is generosity, overflowing life, gratuitousness, unpredictable liberty; who does nothing 'in general', but who is always the 'You' facing that 'I'. Supreme personality in the total gift of himself, he is in the inmost depths of every person, the source of all personality, never alongside human persons, and yet distinct from them. In loving them, I share in his love for them, and I love God himself. He is not something other than created reality (because he is not 'something'): he reveals himself through its contours, its limits and its beauty; however, he is not created reality, but of a different order. He is neither presence nor absence for my senses and intelligence. He is neither more nor less. His true greatness is his humility which impelled him to become man. His wealth is the poverty of love. He has suffered – eternally? – even while being infinite Bliss.

I speak of him, so do I know him? By experience I do not know him. I have not found him among created beings nor seen his imprint in the events of my life, nor found him within me: everything there is created, human, and has its explanation at this level. I cannot express him in words. So all that remains is the face of Christ, human and created, and his Word in Holy Scripture and in the Church (note well that this Word always comes to me through the intermediary of men). Am I finally in the 'truth'? Have I found him in finding him not?

How should I adore such a God?

I said that only the atheist can truly believe in God, for the atheist has nothing but the human. Thus, he can engage his whole being, if he has assumed it fully and lucidly, in an act of faith and a gift of himself which open onto the pure Mystery of a God who is All and Nothing. It is not only God who has vanished, as we were saying: the worshipper has also collapsed under the demoralizing effect of an ever greater lucidity about the complexities and ambiguities of his actions. Little by little, the hidden layers of the psyche are laid bare; the evasions,

the detours of egoism and fear, all the wolves in sheep's clothing, the corruption of the heart which is the very source of all
our actions and prayers. We have to recognize that the pious
lad or lass of former times was only a mask, at least in part;
veneration was an instinctive fear before the invisible and the
judge; obedience, a calculation and a constraint; love, a subjec-
tive emotion produced quite artificially and out of proportion
with its meagre results in real life; austerity, the expression of
a masochistic desire for self-punishment to allay a neurotic
guilt-complex; desire for solitude, the evasion scheme of a crip-
pled personality unable to integrate itself into the life of
humankind.

One could continue indefinitely. What we are saying is obviously exaggerated, yet nonetheless, partly true. Every virtue has
its shadow and is never found in the pure state. Every authentic
movement of the soul has its counterfeit and we are located,
nearly always, somewhere in between the two extremes. All our
human acts are ambiguous.

How can such a one adore?

To pray in spirit and in truth implies that we accept ourselves
in total lucidity just as we are: not passively, crushed by the
weight of a fate from which there is no escape, but with courage
and energy, turning our good qualities to the best account, and
reducing the incursions made by our defects. We have received
the energy of the Spirit of Christ. We should not lose courage
since, in the last analysis, we do not count on a justice of our
own, but on Christ, in faith. He it is who will give us, and
indeed create out of nothing, the good works that give him
glory. It may even be – and this applies particularly, I believe,
to the solitary – that our trust, in spite of our very real poverty,
our desire to love, in spite of the feeble results, our thirst
and our hope, give him the greatest glory. His will is love, and
we have only to espouse it with filial devotion. That is in no
way depressing or servile; on the contrary, it is a true liberation,
since our poverty, in itself, is no asset. But to accept ourselves
as we are is to situate ourselves in the truth, and in the face of
this true self is the love of God which itself is infinitely rich.
Our poverty is the measure of our receptivity, not only with
respect to God's gifts, but with respect to God himself in the

union of love. We should aspire to this poverty as a crystal might seek to be perfectly transparent, in order to become pure light. In love, this poverty is freedom and joy, like God himself. Prayer in spirit and in truth, purity of heart, seeking God, the spirit of the Beatitudes: it is all the same thing, our very life as a monk.

> 'Wash, make yourselves clean.
> Take your wrong-doing out of my sight.
> Cease to do evil.
> Learn to do good . . .
> Though your sins are like scarlet,
> they shall be as white as snow;
> though they are red as crimson,
> they shall be like wool.'
>
> (Isaiah 1:16–18 JB)

18

Seen As We Are*

'For this I was born, and for this I
have come into the world, to bear
witness to the truth. Everyone who
is of the truth hears my voice.'

(John 18:37)

Dear Brothers,

Jesus is standing before Pilate. His life depends on the answers
he gives to the Roman procurator. It is at this moment that he
reveals what seems to be one of the most essential secrets of
his life, for he says: 'For this I was born, and for this I have
come into the world.' At a time when we are celebrating the
birth of our Saviour, it is a good thing for us to know why he
came to us. And it is awesome to discover that he came to bear
witness: that is, to confront each of us with a responsibility that
he has to assume personally, in the depths of his own conscience. What is my attitude to truth going to be?

Jesus does not come to exercise any sort of exterior or interior
compulsion. No, the witness he bears calls for a response that
comes from the heart, and a commitment, not to a system
of ideas, but to a person: to Someone who, in his very being,
is a witness to the Truth, the truth which every human heart
should be ardently seeking. In the presence of the Son of
God, who has just appeared on earth, let us ask ourselves what
our attitude really is towards this truth to which he is bearing
witness before us.

---

*Sermon preached at Christmas.

Jesus made this declaration in answer to Pilate, who was questioning him more and more insistently to find out if he was a king. The judge presses him once again: 'So you are a king?' and Jesus finally answers: 'It is you who say it; yes, I am a king.' What is this kingship of Jesus?

'Anyone who is of the truth listens to my voice,' Jesus says. This is in fact exactly what he had already said in one of his most moving parables: 'My sheep listen to my voice' (John 10: 27). Jesus is king after the manner of a faithful shepherd leading his sheep. 'I am the Good Shepherd; I know my sheep and my sheep know me, just as the Father knows me and I know the Father. And I give my life for my sheep' (John 10:14–15).

Jesus does not exercise his kingship by force, nor by authority, nor by seduction; his sheep follow him freely, because he knows them personally and they know him. It is the same type of knowledge as the mutual knowledge that the Father and the Son have of each other: a knowledge of love.

But we must not forget that it is in the name of truth that the Good Shepherd is drawing his sheep after him. Indeed, it is the Father himself who is drawing them: 'No one can come to me unless the Father who sent me draws him; and I will raise him up on the last day' (John 6: 44). Conversely, Jesus says to the Pharisees who refuse to believe in him: 'He who is of God hears the words of God; the reason why you do not hear them is that you are not of God' (John 8:47).

Christ's testimony is addressed to the light that is shining in every one of us: a light that the Father himself has lit in the inmost centre of our heart. It is not simply the spontaneous attraction to truth that is in us all, but the most personal call made to us by God to seek him and to encounter him. How could this testimony of Jesus be received with anything but enthusiasm?

Yet this is precisely the whole drama of the Gospel. 'The true light that enlightens every man . . . came to his own home, and his own people received him not' (John 1:9–11). 'The light has come into the world, and men loved darkness rather than light, because their deeds were evil' (John 3:19). This is an historical fact. The Witness to the Truth was indeed rejected by his own people who condemned him to death. Jesus was

killed because he testified to the truth, and that is what they
could not tolerate: 'For everyone who does evil hates the light
and does not come to the light, lest his deeds should be
exposed' (John 3:20).

But this is not simply a past event. Do we not see the same
thing happening in our own lives? True, we are not going to
put the Son of God to death because we hate the light, but
how difficult it is for us sometimes to allow the light to flow
into us! It is in the depths of our own hearts that the great
battle between darkness and light is being waged. Why is this?

The reason is simple: 'I know my sheep,' Christ says, 'and
they know me.' If we want to follow our King, we have to
accept being fully and totally known by him; we have to accept
knowing him, unreservedly, as he is. In practical terms, this is
what frightens us.

What does it mean to be known by Jesus? It means accepting
that all should be unveiled, in full light, in his sight and before
our own eyes: our weaknesses and limits, and the whole sum
of infidelities, great and small, that constitute our existence.
Even though, by the mercy of God, we may not be great sinners,
nevertheless there are all sorts of things in our lives that we find
it difficult to look at honestly. Immediately after committing
a fault, especially, we are sometimes extremely unwilling to
acknowledge in the presence of Jesus, honestly and frankly, and
without masks, that we are no more than what we are. That is
why we are afraid of the light.

Think, for example, of the story of the woman taken in
adultery. Jesus simply says to her accusers: 'Let him who is
without sin among you be the first to throw a stone at her'
(John 8:7). And one after another, all of them flee from his
sight. They run far away from him. The only one who remains
in the presence of the Lord is the woman accused who has
now become the woman forgiven, in the light, because she hid
nothing of her poverty from Him. This is the deepest secret of
an intimate relationship with the Lord: we have to allow him
to look at us unreservedly, even if his gaze seems indiscreet, for
in reality it is overflowing with mercy alone.

The other side of the question is that we must know Jesus.
This means accepting him as the one who is asking us to believe

in him: without reserve, taking our hands off the controls, and
with his truth as our only guarantee. We are terribly frightened
of this too. We are so used to assuring our own security ourselves and knowing exactly where we are going, that we are
really afraid of trusting blindly in the Son of God. Absurd
though it may be, our need for tangible security is so great that
we are terrified at the very thought of surrendering ourselves
without defence, even to God himself.

On this count, we can learn from the example of the Pharisees and their endless arguments with the Lord. In the presence
of the God of Israel, they had built up their own personal
justice, and, with their observances and their traditions, they
were completely in control of the whole edifice. Their conscience was at rest before God: 'All that we should have done,
we have done.'

We probably do not go to the same extreme, but we are
exposed to the same sort of temptation in the religious life. Do
we not try to find good, tangible security in observances, in the
reassuring feeling that, thanks to our fidelity, everything is in
order in our relationship with the Lord? And when Jesus asks
us one day to count on him alone, without telling us in advance
what he is going to ask of us, and without explaining to us
where he wants us to go, we tremble.

This is why the testimony of Jesus is not able to bear all the
fruit it should in our lives, even though we do not openly reject
it. We do not listen to his voice as much as he wants us to.

Admitting to this is painful. We feel blocked and paralysed
by our mediocrity and our hesitations. Outwardly our attitude
is fairly correct, but within, the truth does not reach to the
inmost recesses of our heart. So what can I do? Either I remain
paralysed, feeling that I have not the strength to go any further,
and seeing no way out. Or else I can settle for a sort of resigned
scepticism: 'All that is not for me; it is for the great saints, and
I am not a great saint.'

Jesus, however, does not give up on our mediocrity. His only
weapon is truth, but he uses it to the end. Acknowledging our
mediocrity, as we are doing now, and acknowledging it with
humility and sorrow, is in itself a step forward on the path
towards genuine truth. Jesus does not ask me to be a saint in

order to come to him; but he asks me to allow him to know me just as I am, to let him see me in my true light. So we must accept our mediocrity, in the certainty that it does not in any way limit or hamper God's love. Aware I may be of the countless obstacles that I put in the way of the Lord; but to the extent that, even so, I want to place my trust in him, who can prevent him from leading me to the pastures of salvation?

This is what saves me: if I acknowledge all the unfaithfulness and lack of fervour which until now have prevented me from trusting in God and held me back from letting myself be known by him; if I acknowledge this and allow myself to be known by God just as he is, in his freely given mercy, then I experience at last and for always, the truth of Christ. He alone will give me life; as for me, I can only bring my weakness. 'My sheep hear my voice,' Jesus says, 'and I know them and they follow me: and I give them eternal life' (John 10:27).

To conclude these reflections, let us admit how easy it would be for us to receive the truth that is coming to us today, if only we were poor enough to acknowledge that we have nothing. We would like to have something worthy to give to God, whereas St John tells us just the contrary: 'In this is love: not that we loved God, but that he loved us, and sent his Son to be the expiation for our sins' (John 4:10). Just as the Son receives everything from the Father, we too must receive everything from the Son, so that he may offer us in joy to his Father. Amen.

19

The Journey to Purity of Heart

Blessed are the pure in heart, for they shall see God.
(Matthew 5:8)

Dear Brothers,

The angel's greeting to Mary is an inexhaustible subject for meditation: 'Rejoice, you who enjoy God's favour: the Lord is with you' (Luke 1:28 NJB). This summons to the most pure Virgin to rejoice, because she is perfectly ready to receive the gift of the Most High, evokes the Beatitudes, in which Jesus invites us also to receive that joy, to the extent that we too make ourselves transparent to the work of God in us. Let us today reflect in particular on the Beatitude of the pure in heart, following the most ancient monastic tradition. For did not monks of earlier centuries regard purity of heart as the ultimate goal towards which their asceticism was directed? And were not the words of Jesus in fact a transposition of the angel's greeting? The only perfect purity of heart is the fullness of grace of the Mother of God; to say to Mary that the Lord is with her signifies that she sees God. Hence, the Virgin Mary alone completely fulfils the Beatitude of the pure in heart, which is why only she can truly teach us about it. So let us today, in the light of her Immaculate Conception, try to meditate as best we can on this inexhaustible theme.

None of us has a pure heart spontaneously; if we attain it one day, it will be at the cost of great effort. Thus, it is primarily a question for us aspiring to purify our hearts. Our first concern is therefore to show the way of this purification: through what stages will we have to pass that our hearts may become as clear waters which will reflect the image of God?

Jesus has a terrible observation to make about our impure hearts: 'Whatever comes out of the mouth comes from the heart, and it is this that makes someone unclean. For from the heart come evil intentions: murder, adultery, fornication, theft, perjury, slander. These are the things that make a person unclean' (Matthew 15:18–20 NJB). Our hearts arc the source of the pollution which spreads through both our inner and outer selves. In the very centre of our life of prayer there is an inexhaustible reservoir of disturbance, noise, agitation and of fog clouding our eyes as we seek the divine light. That is the heart we have to purify.

It would be foolish to want to deal at a stroke with this source of impurity without first disposing of all those external actions which make us blind. The first stage on the journey to purity of heart is interior silence. To ensure that our actions regain a genuine integrity, and above all to bring order into our thoughts and imaginations: this is the first, indispensable purification if we want to rediscover our hearts, hidden and buried as they are by the rush and bustle within us.

And so, one day we finally succeed in establishing silence within ourselves. But it is too early to proclaim victory, for we still find ourselves in the presence of that inexhaustible source that I spoke of earlier. We have to experience the painful reality of our impure hearts: even if our imagination has fallen silent and our thoughts become stilled, we shall find in the depths of ourselves a kind of fundamental instability, an inexhaustible fount of anxiety, a seedbed of judgements, condemnations and fear. If we are truly to have a strong desire to purify this heart, we must first experience its impurity and feel the radical need to transform it, if we are one day to see God.

This, then, is the next stage in our journey: to seek to purify the waters of our interior source. That means, first of all, custody of the heart, as that beautiful classical formula puts it: not allowing it to be agitated by all those circumstances which we know will give rise to unhealthy emotions, anxiety and distraction. We must establish a prudent control of our feelings; we must renounce superficiality so as to remain attentive to the deep movements within our heart, since we now know that it is from there that all our trouble proceeds. And so, little by little, the waters of that source will purify themselves. Yet we shall often be tempted to lose heart when our efforts appear inadequate to the task we have set ourselves.

By the time we have reached this stage in the purification of our heart, it is clear that we shall never transform it sufficiently by our own efforts to make it worthy of receiving the light from on high. It is then that we make our own, as though addressed to us personally, the word that God spoke to Israel through Ezekiel:

> 'I shall pour clean water over you and you will be cleansed; I shall cleanse you of all your filth and of all your foul idols. I shall give you a new heart, and put a new spirit in you; I shall remove the heart of stone from your bodies and give you a heart of flesh instead. I shall put my spirit in you, and make you keep my laws, and respect and practise my judgements.' (Ezekiel 36: 25–27 NJB)

If the Lord himself gets involved, how can we doubt that our hearts will in the end be totally transformed? This is the light that shines in the darkness and puts it to flight; this is the silence of God that is louder than all the sounds of creation. But it must be emphasized that such a transformation will never be acquired cheaply. It is, in fact, the transposition, on the level of hearts, of what Jesus experienced when he bore the sin of the world before the Father, that is, its defilement, its utter absence of silence. In order to enter the repose of God, we must first pass through the trial which will transform us from within.

But the words of Ezekiel go much further. It is not just a matter of cleansing our hearts; it is in the end a matter of recognizing that the ultimate defilement which taunts us is precisely that we do not have a heart at all. It is a stone complacently wallowing in the world of its own emotions that we have instead. Turned in on itself, how could it ever open itself to God and attain the transparency necessary for the light to penetrate it through and through? For as long as I have a stone for a heart, how can I not remain closed off from my brother and thus cut off from the One whose image he is?

Give us, then, Lord, a heart of flesh: a fragile, vulnerable heart, attentive to all you say to it. Instead of this unfeeling and lifeless stone, give us a heart which knows how to respond, to suffer if necessary, and above all, to give itself to you.

'I shall remove the heart of stone from your bodies and give you a heart of flesh instead,' says the prophet. In other words, it is in my sensing and material self that God wishes to dwell. The Incarnate Word has come to meet me in the depths of my human nature, however unresponsive that nature might appear. In fact, in the eyes of God, that nature is not impure at all: it is precisely because I had denied its fragility that it became hard as stone. So if I want to possess the heart that God means me to have, I must allow myself to be exposed to all the assaults from the outside and to resonate with the sufferings of my brothers, sensitive to everything that affects them, so as to be equally responsive to all that affects God and to all that comes from him. My heart must become the place in which resounds the vibrant echo of all that is most intimate in the heart of my brother.

In the light of all this, we will surely be tempted to say, as did the Virgin: 'But how can this come about?' (Luke 1:34). Are we not talking about a distant and inaccessible ideal? No. God stepped right across the distance which separates us from him when he sent us his Son. It is now up to us to encounter this Divine Word made flesh. When that happens, his heart and mine come together. Through the human relationships which he wanted to create between each of us and himself, through this extraordinary intimacy that we possess with him who is a human being like us, the encounter to which we aspire takes place; it is his heart which will transform mine and make it capable of contemplating God. 'The one who sees me sees the Father,' he says. This is the secret which he has entrusted to us: if our eyes of flesh know how to see the Son, our heart will be transformed and will look upon God.

This is also the promise made to us by Ezekiel, when he announced the coming of a new Spirit, the Spirit which Jesus gave us definitively after he had been glorified. If he does not yet hold sway in us, it is because we do not thirst for him enough. 'Let anyone who is thirsty come to me! Let anyone who believes in me come and drink!' As Scripture says, ' "From his heart shall flow streams of living water," ' (John 7:37-38). This is what must become of the defiled source which flows in us now. It must become a pure source; for, as the Gospel goes on to say: 'Jesus was speaking of the Spirit which those who believed in him were to receive' (John 7:39). This is the ultimate transformation to which our hearts are called: to be the well from which the Spirit springs forth.

We feel overwhelmed by these reflections: they seem so far above us! And yet, are they not directly concerned with promises that Jesus has made to each and every one of us? So why view them as strange? Let us simply ask the Virgin Mary, in conclusion, to give us an attitude of true humility, whereby we will have a genuine thirst for Jesus. Not only did she possess a heart of flesh, but she bore in her flesh the very Son of God himself. May she lead us out of shadow towards the Light which is the blessed fruit of her womb.

20

'Encourage One Another'

Brothers,

As planned during the preparatory phase, the pastoral programme of the General Chapter included a reflection, in small
groups and in the Assembly, on initiation into the life of prayer
at all stages (in the novitiate and afterwards). We consider this
reflection to have been extremely useful. It alerted us to a
certain number of problems, and allowed the capitulants to
share the fruit of their own experience. It underscored, in particular, how important it is, on our pilgrimage, to have the help
of a brother, or of an 'elder', and it was our desire that this
charism should develop within the Order.

We hope to be able to disseminate these reflections more
widely, by means of a summary to be printed later.

And now, gathered together as we are on the site where our
Father St Bruno lived, we would like to say to all our brothers
in the Order: 'Let us rejoice . . . in the generous outpouring of
God's grace on us; let us always give thanks to God the Father'
for all the gifts of prayer that he has showered upon us throughout the centuries. And to all those who labour and stumble
along the tortuous paths of prayer, we say, with all the affection
that the Spirit inspires in our hearts: do not hesitate to continue
your journey, or to take it up again, even if you have the
impression of gathering no fruit.

Remember that our prayer is not the result of our own efforts,
but of the Spirit in our hearts. It is a long journey between
ourselves and the One who is completely Other. It implies a
radical purification, the transformation of our entire being in

God, after the image of Christ. For us, this can only be a
path of poverty and hope. A hope that is obscure and dark, but
full of joy, 'for God is greater than our hearts' (1 John 3:20).

IV

The Vows

STABILITY

21

Perseverance in the Crucible

The monk, who continues faithfully in his cell and lets himself be moulded by it, will gradually find that his whole life tends to become one continual prayer. But he cannot attain to this repose except at the cost of stern battle; both by living austerely in fidelity to the law of the Cross, and willingly accepting the tribulations by which God will try him as gold in the furnace. In this way, having been cleansed in the night of patience, and having been consoled and sustained by assiduous meditation of the Scriptures, and having been led by the Holy Spirit into the depths of his own soul, he is now ready, not only to serve God, but even to cleave to him in love.

(Statutes 3.2)

As indicated in this text, the work of purification has two aspects, one active, the other passive. The active purification is that which we undertake on our own initiative, following Christ 'in fidelity to the law of the Cross'. It is a way of conforming ourselves to Christ: poor, chaste and obedient, and of sharing in his suffering for the love of our brothers: the prayer of blood.

Let us look at this a little more closely. The life of the senses is good; the senses are the windows of the soul. Pleasure is necessary to life. Sensitivity is a powerful asset, provided it is kept in its right place within human life as a whole, and subject to mind and will. Otherwise it is a blind force and destructive of the person as such. Good servant, bad master.

In actual fact, self-discipline is necessary in order to bring our sensitive life into harmony with the intellectual and spiritual life, and to transform our sensual appetites into spiritual desires. This cannot be achieved without a certain experience of deprivation. Therein lies the spiritual value of fasting and temperance, and it is the price to be paid for basic human freedom.

Self-assertion is a good thing; its complete absence would be a malady. But we are inclined to put self at the centre of everything. We perceive everything as revolving around ourselves, as valuable only in so far as it brings us some advantage. In short, we are born self-centred and superficial. To put Christ at the centre of everything, to see everything, including ourselves, in relation to him, to love and to act in the light of this perspective, involves a death to self and a deep transformation of our heart. We have to acquire humility, and this is a most difficult task.

Obedience helps here by combating our pride and spirit of independence; we learn humility by conforming our will to that of God, made known in the Church through a human voice.

Poverty is also a help in this respect by attacking our tendency to self-inflation through possessions and our covetousness. Lastly, the discipline of faith helps towards this end by weaning our intellect from its natural objects and light.

It is always a question of passing from disordered self-love to the love of God. Chastity bears directly on the purification of our affections by easing the passage from a narcissistic love of self and self-centred love of another, to a love that is a gift of self to the other and God. All this applies to the spiritual man in general. As regards the life of prayer, solitude, silence, *lectio divina*, the constant directing of our attention to the Lord, the endeavour to remain recollected: these little by little purify the heart.

We have chosen to live on the manna in the desert; we must be content with it despite the lack of taste our human faculties sometimes find in it. A thousand times we have to 'return', that is, to choose the general and obscure light of a gaze directed towards the realities of faith rather than towards things more immediately accessible. An expectant gaze, but free from preconceptions. A welcoming gaze for what is and always will be beyond, for the mystery within the infinitely near. A loving gaze, which chooses, which desires to love. A thousand small acts which deepen the streams of our desire and purify the heart.

Purification means passage, Passover: ever to pass beyond, beyond consolations and lights, natural or supernatural, beyond dryness and darkness. It means abandonment of every possession in the movement towards the One who awaits us, there behind the screen. It is trust in his love, and desire to return that love. It entails an exchange of friendship, and what friendship! Intimate communion with the Holy Trinity, a communion which is my only good. Our choice must respond to his, person to person, heart to heart. It implies an untiring effort, constantly renewed, to tear myself from the superficial and immerse myself . . . in what? In being, in myself, in God? At least in reality. And thus we come to control of the imagination: intimately dependent on sense impression, the imagination too can be a good servant when used with discretion and under strict control. But as a master, it never fails to lead us astray in the moral sphere and especially in the interior life. Purification, then, means the difficult ascesis of living the present moment. It is the acceptance of my finitude and of my death. It is ability to receive, openness to love.

Once we have seen the work of purification to be accomplished, we give ourselves to it with all our good will. Sooner or later, however, we begin to realize that what we can achieve by ourselves, even with the help of grace* is limited. Our scrutiny reaches only the surface of things; the deep roots of our heart escape it to a large extent, and our knowledge of God (it is the love of God that inspires our whole undertaking) is obscure and partial. As a result, our will remains weak and inconstant, easily seduced by outward goods, constantly deceived by the imagination, unable of itself to break completely the bonds of egocentric self-love. Despite everything,

---

*From the theological point of view our activity is always the fruit of the grace and power of the Spirit within us. Passivity is always first; but the psychological mode can be active or passive according to circumstances.

we are our own masters, and our ascetic activity can be an additional possession which serves to foster a subtle complacency and spiritual pride.

In short, our activity is inadequate because of the means at our disposal and the fact that it is ours. How then is the Christ life in us to be released? Only by the action of God himself. All that is asked of us is our 'yes' to this action, our free consent. This is the passive purification, the 'visits of the Lord' of which the Statutes speak.

Like Peter, each of us will hear addressed to himself, sooner or later, the words of Christ indicating the condition of all spiritual fruitfulness: 'Feed my lambs,' he said to Peter.

> 'I tell you most solemnly,
> when you were young
> you put on your own belt
> and walked where you liked;
> but when you grow old
> you will stretch out your hands,
> and somebody else will put a belt round you
> and take you where you would rather not go.'
>
> In these words he indicated the kind of death by which Peter would give glory to God. (John 21:17–19 JB)

Somebody else will take you where you would rather not go. This is how the Lord frees us from ourselves and centres us once more on his will and his love.

PASSIVE PURIFICATIONS

We should not think of two successive periods of time. The Lord is directly at work in our souls from the outset. Nevertheless, one can admit that the active purification is usually predominant in the first stages of the spiritual life and the passive purification later.

A distinction can be drawn between purifications which come from without and those which come from within. The Statutes speak of the first in the following terms:

We are well aware how much patience and perseverance in the situation in which God has placed us contribute to contemplation of things divine. For, it is not possible for a man to keep his mind firmly fixed on one person if, beforehand, he has not perseveringly kept his body in one place. And if the mind is to draw near to him in whom there is neither change nor shadow of alteration, it must adhere unshakenly to its undertaking. (30.8)

'Patience and perseverance in the situation in which God has placed us.' The word 'situation' comprises everything that forms the framework of our life: persons, things, events big and small. 'In which God has placed us.' What exists and is real is willed by God and included within the design of his providence. The persons God puts at my side, the place, the time, health and sickness, the play of events, all of that moulds and forms me, oppresses me or lifts me up, makes me rebellious or sanctifies me.

The essential thing is to recognize the will of God here, to accept it with the suppleness of the reed blown by the wind, not shutting myself up within the frail confines of my own wisdom, but letting myself be moulded by the all-powerful hands of the Creator.

Easy to say, hard indeed to live. Patience and perseverance are forms of passivity, the fruit of great force and great faith. It is not resignation but the deliberate embracing of a dearly loved will: an act of love all the purer in that it has only one thing to say: *fiat.* Yes, may your will be done on earth as it is in heaven, Father; your will, not mine.

Christ saw his executioners as agents of his Father's will. We in our turn must learn to see this same will, this same love, in all the circumstances, pleasant or unpleasant, that surround our life.

We come to the monastery as to an ideal place in which all is planned and ordered in function of the search for God, and for the full blossoming out of love towards God and our brothers. Such is our expectation; but we carry within us a very idealized picture of its realization. And so things turn out differently. There are those who come in search of tranquillity,

shelter, a quiet life; on the contrary, they find themselves struggling with forces within themselves whose existence they never
suspected. Our faults are a barrier; our brothers are imperfect
and different from us; sin affects our relationships; the institution is ponderous and opaque; and God seems to take a
malicious pleasure in thwarting our ideas.

In fact he is doing us the great service of stripping us of
much of our egoism and childishness, of our attachments and
disordered desires. In so doing he separates the sheep from the
goats. Only when the secondary benefits we expected from our
vocation are seen to be more or less illusory, can the essential
aim, union with God, be embraced in all its purity – otherwise
one leaves.

Perseverance in such a situation is conducive to contemplation, for we find ourselves poor and naked before the Lord,
ready at last to receive the incomprehensible gift which he
wishes to give us, and not a construct of our own imagination.
Moreover, 'if you knew the gift of God' (John 3:10), you would
ask for this poverty and accept it with joy.

To stand firm, however, in certain painful circumstances can
demand much courage: the long night of waiting, the loneliness
of not being understood, unjust treatment, poor health, personal defects, etc. We have to know how to stand firm in pure
faith when we seem to be only weakness, seem to be only sin.
We have to consent in advance to all that, to the desert of the
desert. We have to desire the purity which suffering alone can
teach.

It seems to me perseverance is a great school of humility: a
gradual coming to know this self which persists in time, whose
features become defined, whose character traits recur, whose
limits take shape. Through trial one discovers one's own heart,
and becomes an authentic person situated in the real.

The great strength of humility lies in its never giving way to
despair. Despair* is often the offspring of pride, the feeling
of resentment when an over-inflated self-image bursts upon
exposure to the light. The humble man falls; he does not always

---

*I speak here of despair from the point of view of passive spiritual purifi-
cation, not of the subject in its entire breadth.

succeed, but he always begins again, patiently and with tenacity. Perseverance is not something static. It is the ever-creative recovery of precarious balance, the re-focusing of a trajectory constantly exposed to the attraction of forces which tend to deflect it from its orbit. Considerable creativity is necessary to sustain the melody of one's life within a life-setting as severe and specific as ours.

Stagnation and sclerosis are a betrayal of true perseverance. It is to stop in one's tracks, to become immobilized in formulas which have been effective in times past, to cling to a self-image which gives us security, to quench the Spirit.

Meanwhile we are at times reduced to a material or animal perseverance, or even to simply being there, like a rock, without really knowing why, nor to what purpose. It is like a narrow room without light or air. Still, one goes on by a sort of gravitational law. Later, one realizes that perseverance is a pure grace, independent of any personal merit. Then, the Spirit once again breathes life into our dried bones; we get up and go on.

Let us not forget that we live at a site of quite extraordinary perseverance.* The stones in our buildings bear witness to a will to stand firm in the face of snow and ice, catastrophe upon catastrophe, avalanche, fire, revolutions; a monastery that rebuilds itself almost every century through eight centuries – no slight thing! What a cloud of witnesses surrounds us and encourages us!

A man who does not know how to persevere, to bring to completion what he has begun, will never achieve anything worthwhile in his life. The plant that is continually displaced does not take root; it does not grow and bears no fruit. The hairs of our head are numbered. Since Divine Providence governs everything, how much more the life of those whose sole aim is to seek the Lord!

Let us think of what makes up our life – our familial, psychological and social inheritance – as the materials given us to create a work of art. A masterpiece is not such because it is made of expensive material, but because of the beauty it expresses. A marvellous sketch can be made with a bit of

---

*The Grande Chartreuse.

charcoal. Poverty of means is a challenge to our ingenuity. The merit is all the greater if the material is poor. The artist knows precisely how to exploit its limitations, to make it the expression of his spirit. Let us not waste time in regrets that we are not marble but granite. Even the lack of means, the absence of certain gifts, can lead us to discover and use to advantage the empty space in the architecture of our house.

Let us build with what has been given us, with the real in its irreducible particularity. Time – my short span of life – is part of the reality: my age as well, being born in this century and in such and such a year. My place: this country, this town, this school, this house. My blood: this race, this colour, this family, this father, this mother, these brothers and sisters. My heart: this love, these friends and enemies. The web of passing events: these encounters, these contacts, this door open, that window shut, at the very moment I was passing. Intersecting footprints on the virgin snow of a history ever new for me.

Let us take all this and construct our house. Let us build on what is solid: on Christ. There is no other foundation. What is more, let us build Christ himself (cf. Ephesians 4:12ff.) who is the image of God.

22

Stability in the Resurrection*

**When they saw the star,
the wise men rejoiced with great joy.
Matthew (2:10)**

Dear Father,

Before recounting the adoration of the magi, the Gospel tells us about the adversities they faced on their way to Jesus. When they reached Jerusalem, their guiding star disappeared; after searching, they were finally told by Herod that they were to go farther, in direction of Bethlehem. It was then that the star reappeared and came to rest above the place where the Child Jesus was lying. We have here, in the perseverance of these men, an example of constancy and of determination to attain a precise aim, greater than the obstacles which could have drawn them away from it. As you prepare to take your solemn vows, I would like to see in this an example of monastic stability. For there is more to this stability than the simple notion of perpetual vows, and it is well worth our spending a few minutes thinking about it.

Why should we take a vow of stability? We learn that this practice began quite early in the history of monasticism; it was seen as a necessary part of the attitude of a monk who chooses to give himself to God irrevocably, so as to have no other aim on earth but him. The reason is very simple: a multitude of possibilities are continually exercising attraction over our human nature which has to choose from among them, and this

*Sermon preached on the Feast of the Epiphany, for a Final Profession.

is a source of hesitation, anxiety and error. If we want to progress, step by step, and come nearer to God, we need a force within us to keep us unswervingly directed towards him.

We have the example of Jesus and Mary themselves: they had to contend with situations in which they hesitated, in which some kind of obscurity prevented them from seeing immediately the right path to take, even though they had no doubts about what their aim was. Mary was surprised by the message of the angel; she spent three days looking for Jesus in the Temple, without understanding what was happening; one day Jesus told his relatives that he would not be going to Jerusalem, and then the very next day he set off for the town . . .

For us sinners, the situation is even less clear: our soul is always more or less in darkness, because it is not in perfect harmony with God. This makes our choices even more difficult, and perseverance in the decisions we have taken uncertain. Inevitably, we run the risk either of not finding the right direction, or else, under the pretext of not losing it, of not seeing the turnoffs that Providence has arranged for us. That is why, whenever we are tending towards some distant and difficult target, we need to have within us the ability to remain firmly turned in the right direction.

This then is what stability is. But we must not imagine it to be some sort of immobility, or the unchanging rigidity of stone or mountain. Stability is a human attitude: a fidelity. It is a living fidelity: that is, a manifestation of life, in the concrete conditions in which it has to develop. We have an example of stability in the victorious force of a seed cast into the ground: through what appears to be decomposition, and struggling with all kinds of obstacles which it transforms into means, it becomes a plant that grows and develops according to the laws of its nature, and eventually bears fruit. Doesn't Jesus compare the kingdom of heaven to a mustard seed? This is the fidelity of the Church: starting with a little group of Galileans, fishermen on the lake of Genesareth, it has become a society of millions of people from all over the world, from every culture and every sphere of human activity, now living in communion with one another.

Stability takes us beyond the fascination of multiplicity: it makes us concentrate our efforts in such a way that we can advance, in depth, in one chosen direction, the one we know to be right for the life in which we are engaged. It centres us on that point from which we know that light will flare. So monastic life will receive its stability from God himself. All our activities, all our interior energy, are to be channelled towards him, whereas the paths that risk drawing us away from him are to be left aside. This is the goal, then: to press forward in the hope of reaching God himself one day, because his Word has given us the certitude that we can do so. But how are we to reach this goal?

First, it must be pointed out that stability is not a specifically monastic attitude. There exists what could be called a Christian stability, that is, fidelity to our being Christian. It has its source in the one and only perfect and permanent stability, the only human life which reached this goal without fault or error, through the winding paths of an existence full of trouble and contradiction: that of the risen Christ. Such is the glorious stability towards which we tend and which we wish to share. Is not this the meaning of the motto of our Order: *Stat Crux dum volvitur orbis*? Not the material stability of the Cross as an instrument of torture, but the eternal permanence of the Resurrection to which it gives access.

It is through baptism that we are conformed to Jesus in his Resurrection: this is the foundation of our Christian stability. Baptism implies a commitment to tend towards the Resurrection; it is already a radical participation in the Resurrection that we must develop, like the mustard seed. Baptism commits us to this, but at the same time it gives the strength necessary for this new being grafted onto our nature to reach its full development.

In practice, it is through our belonging to the Church that the stability of life, to which we are invited by baptism, is realized. For, if we are able to follow the way initially chosen, it is not because of our personal strength, or because of some personal interior grace of which we might have the conrol. To be faithful to our baptism, we have to live in rhythm with the Church; we have to belong to the community of Christians, by letting ourselves draw support from it and be guided by it. It is always in relationship with our brothers that we find the light and strength we need to move forward towards our goal.

It is the same with monastic stability. The official sign of this stability is the Profession that you are about to make. This Profession is acknowledged by the Church and it is the explicit teaching of the Council that religious profession is a prolongation of baptism, a means of being faithful to it in a more radical and effective way. It is a sign of the Resurrection of Jesus, and witnesses in advance to the fruits of the Resurrection. So we can be quite sure of this: Profession is a continuation of Christian stability; it grafts us onto our risen Lord Jesus.

However, no more than baptism can Profession of itself compensate for our weakness, or make up for our lack of light. Our Profession, it is true, represents a commitment of the Holy Spirit to help us by his grace, to send us his light, and to communicate his strength to us. But there is more. The chief visible effect of our Profession is that it incorporates us permanently into the house. We become members of the community; we enter into the communion of all the professed members of the house. It is this communion in its transparency that lets us know what God wants of us, and is the means he gives us to reach our chosen aim: that is, to be as perfectly as possible in communion with the divine Persons.

Our monastic stability and our membership of the community are therefore completely linked. If this centred, in-depth path, of which we were speaking earlier, is really the one we want to take, if we want to remain stably turned in direction of our aim, then we must let ourselves be adopted fully and unreservedly by the community; in a way, we must let ourselves be absorbed by it, even though we may feel that we are losing part of our autonomy, our independence of choice. This death is the price to be paid if we are to enter into the Resurrection of Christ, as proposed to us in the communion of our brothers. In particular, the Statutes, which give us the concrete form of life we are to follow, come to us from the community. And this exterior observance is meaningful when it is interpreted, in each concrete circumstance, not by our own will or personal tastes, but by tradition, which again comes to us through the community.

Finally, it is in the Prior that the community finds its unity. The servant of his brothers, he is taken from among them to be the imperfect, but very real sign of the sole centre of authentic unity: the risen Christ. At the heart of the community, it is the Prior who is the guarantee of our stability.

So, in short, this stability is not some fine theory that can be drawn up in advance: it is daily fidelity to the community, humble and continued obedience to the Prior or to those delegated by him to direct us. Thus it enables us to reflect in our own life the image of Jesus, on his way to the Father in a human existence, subject to all sorts of questions, difficulties and risks, but unified in his obedience to the One who sent him.

We must bring these reflections to an end. Stability is a precious gift to you from the Lord. It will allow you to tend towards him with exceptional security and speed. But do not forget that by your Profession you become a member of the community in a total and definitive way: and so, in communion with all your brothers, you too become responsible for the stability of others. We are accountable in this way for the life of our brothers, for they are guided by the community, and we are the community. We must be aware of this responsibility, but let us know too how to assume it with humility in the presence of the Lord. For this was Jesus' last prayer to his Father: 'May they be one ... that the world may know that you have loved them even as you have loved me' (John 17:23). It is by the unity reigning among us, the charity, the mutual self-giving, that together we will become a sign of the love of the Father, a light that will guide each of us towards the glorious day of the Resurrection. Amen.

23

Our 'Yes' Through the Years

The call of God is not something isolated, an event that took place at a given moment and is placed totally in the past. Of course, we are conscious of the call as a privileged moment in time, but the call itself is a creative word of God which springs forth from eternity. That first moment when we are aware of the call is never exhausted in meaning: it continues to resonate throughout our life and only reveals its depths in the totality of our living and being. Our 'Yes' to the call has, therefore, a story – a story that we cannot foresee unfolding in advance.

We must not see the call as a reality completely determined beforehand, programmed, like a disk inserted into a computer according to our first 'Yes'. Then, without error, the machine does the rest. Rather, we are questioned each moment, entreated by the Spirit to advance further all the time on an unknown path. We must remain always in the attitude of one who is called, who follows the Master in the renewed beginnings of each day. As the Servant of the Lord says:

The Lord has given me
a disciple's tongue.
So that I may know how to reply to the wearied he provides
    me with speech.
Each morning he wakes me to hear,
to listen like a disciple.
The Lord has opened my ear.
For my part, I made no resistance.

(Isaiah 50:4–5 JB)

Our fidelity to the Spirit is expressed over the years in a dynamic fidelity: a 'yes' to God is always open and available.

How, then, commit myself to a future that I do not know and cannot control? Is this not to hinder the action of the Spirit and freeze movement in our life? The answer to this question can only be found in God. It is he who has called us to give ourselves completely in a particular commitment. It is the Spirit who urges us on. It is to the Lord that we commit ourselves even if we cannot know in clear detail all that this commitment involves. For this we can only abandon ourselves to God in total confidence, knowing that what he has begun in us he will bring to completion.

GOD'S FIDELITY

It is God who is, in the first place, committed to us. His unshakeable faithfulness is the basis of our fidelity. The Lord is our rock, our fortress, our shield, and he cannot deny himself. When faced with our infidelity he remains faithful (Romans 3:3): his fidelity does not depend on ours. 'God, by calling you has joined you to his son, Jesus Christ; and God is faithful' (1 Corinthians 1:9). 'You can trust God not to let you be tried beyond your strength' (1 Corinthians 10:13 JB).

God reveals Himself in the Bible as the Living God who is, and who will be, with his people in their struggles, and as the one who will be faithful to his promises and his covenant (see Deuteronomy 7:7, 11). His fidelity consists in loving with an irreversible tenderness and an unfailing love. He binds his strength to man's weakness, in whom against all reason, God has confidence. Indeed, God runs the risk of uniting his name and his being to an unsteady partner. That God is faithful characterizes not only his own unchanging being but his historical and irrevocable choices. His fidelity is revealed by his deeds in history and by his covenant, even to the Incarnation and death of his Son. It is an eternal creation which continually springs forth anew. His fidelity, like his being, is for us a mystery, and the expressions it takes astounds us. Often it embraces our complexity and writes straight with crooked lines.

Man, on the other hand, is subject to time in the sense that he grows and develops within its confines: he does not arrive complete. Yet he is above time in that he can free himself from it and, by his thought, link the past to the future, and so commit himself to that which is yet to come. Man transcends the sheer movement of becoming and gives it a meaning.

His fidelity is consistency with a meaning he has given his life in a moment of time. His truth is not necessarily the spontaneity of the present moment, taken in limitation and isolation, but that which follows from the choice and commitment in the depths of his being: a commitment that triumphs over the fragmentation of time and gives unity and coherence to his life.

Such was the effect of the *Fiat* of Mary. It matured in her as the Word himself, during the long years of the simple, hidden life of Nazareth, through pondering the sometimes enigmatic events of the life of Jesus (the Presentation in the Temple, the three days when Jesus stayed with the doctors, Cana). It matured as perfect docility to the ever-growing light during the public ministry of her Son; by her faithful presence at the foot of the cross; by her place in the heart of the Church waiting for the Holy Spirit. It was only when the fruit was completely matured that the Lord took her to his side in glory.

DAILY LIFE

It is not moments of exaltation, even dramatic religious experiences which happen to us, that are the most important in our monastic life. It is perseverance in daily prayer that is the most important: daily fidelity to the state we have chosen; the constant effort to live for the Lord in the Spirit of his love throughout the day, throughout this day. It is possible that this steadfastness conceals a mystery of hardship and poverty. It is difficult to allow ourselves to be fashioned by God in such a way that we renounce all turning back, that at a given moment we simply entrust the unfolding of our life to God, in all that has been achieved and for all that is yet to be. To persevere in an attitude of receptive waiting, without anxiety, without forcing the end: nothing more. This can be the expression of a more personal bond with Christ, of a radical faith: to give to him one's total being in order that, uncontrolled and uncontrollable, he will do with us as he wishes. Subsequently this attitude makes us capable of an ever-greater abandonment which loses, more and more, all ambition of personal fulfilment. This bears more profoundly the seal of the Son's abandonment to his Father, and fills humanity with his redeeming grace, the love which is the life of the Holy Trinity.

THE TREE

'A blessing on the man who puts his trust in Yahweh, with
   Yahweh for his hope.
He is like a tree by the waterside
that thrusts its roots to the stream:
when the heat comes, it feels no alarm,
its foliage stays green;
it has no worries in a year of drought,
and never ceases to bear fruit.'

(Jeremiah 17:7–8 JB)

It is first of all an acorn which falls from the tree. It is small and, in company with other young acorns, carried here and there according to the whim of the wind in its capricious dance. It is independent, free, light and under the sun, full of promise but fickle, a little irresponsible, we might say. Thus it journeys far, sees many things from outside without committing itself. Then one day, it has to take responsibility for the life it bears within itself. It finds a space, a place where it can grow. It roots itself, alone, in the dark earth. It disappears, it seems to die; but it is more a question of transformation. It loses the shell which protected it in its youth, the heart of its being is laid bare, vulnerable, without light, but thus rendered capable of drawing nourishment from the earth for its life. It adapts little by little to this new kind of existence; it spread out its roots to the sources of life and draws from there its strength. Its being expands and opens, attracted by the light. It thrusts a fragile shoot towards the sun which gives it warmth. It arrays itself in fresh and tender foliage and is no longer alone. It sees other young trees, its brothers, which grow around it. It breathes forth its joy in prayer. It presses its mouth to the earth in order to draw from it its substance. Its arms open to the sky to welcome the rain, warmth, light. It joins earth to heaven in a mutuality of living: its being is its prayer.

It stands firm in its place, bending before the storm, then standing upright. Obediently it embraces the annual rhythm of the life and death of the seasons. It lets itself be stripped by the winds of winter, affected by the cold, the ice. It spreads under heaven its pointed limbs, naked and black. It withstands the long barrenness of winter by withdrawing into itself and patiently waiting.

When the earth awakens, the sap rises in the tree. It adorns itself in fresh foliage which shelters the birds; the buds appear and grow, the flower blossoms, the fruit forms in the sun. In all simplicity, it gives to the good and bad without distinction, what it has received. It shelters everyone in its shade. When its fruits are ripe, the first to come may gather them. It keeps nothing for itself. By the simple fact of being there, it gentles the violence of the seasons, strengthens the earth around it, preventing erosion. The best of its substance passes into its seed and forms the acorns that it then throws freely to the adventure of living. It does not resist the ageing of autumn. It clothes itself with gentle colours. Its leaves die, covering the soil with a sumptuous carpet. It enters yet again into the season of death, silently, and in faith, a witness to permanence in the flux of time.

CONVERSION

24

To Create is to Forget

Today I am going to try not simply to communicate some ideas to you, but rather to share with you an experience – or better, a way of living – that is utterly central and important for me. I shall make use of words and images, but only in order to evoke another level of reality which I invite you to enter. We shall therefore begin with a period of silence, for it is silence which will be the place of our communion.

Let each person settle himself in a relaxed position, but remaining fully awake. Close your eyes. Enter into yourselves. Become fully conscious of your body; welcome the rhythm of your breathing, and slow it down a little. Let yourself be fully and serenely there, from the centre of your being to its exterior. You are. Let us stay together, like that, in silence, for a moment.

I now want to speak to you. I ask you to listen to me at the level of your inmost being, with the ear of your silence. I shall leave some spaces in the reading. Allow what these words evoke to live in your hearts.

I want to know Christ and the power of his resurrection and the sharing of his sufferings by becoming like him in his death, if somehow I may attain the resurrection from the dead. Not that I have already obtained this or have already reached the goal; but I press on to make it my own, because Christ Jesus has made me his own. Beloved, I do not consider that I have made it my own; but this one thing I do: forgetting what lies behind and straining forward to what lies ahead, I press on toward the goal for the prize of the heavenly call of God in Christ Jesus. (Philippians 3:10–14 NRSV)

'Forgetting what lies behind and straining forward to what lies ahead, I press on toward the goal . . .'

Profession, whether simple or solemn, cannot be an end in an absolute sense. It is an end with regard to the past; it is a point of departure with regard to the future. And Paul insists on saying that we must be straining forward to what lies ahead. The road that lies behind is to be forgotten: no more useless regrets, no more 'if only's', no complacency about the spiritual riches we have accumulated.

In the presence of God, we are always unworthy servants, forgiven sinners, poor men. We are not to close our hands on empty space, but keep them open towards the Lord in order to receive the generosity of his love. We are sons and daughters to the extent to which we are born of God; and we are born naked.

The power of forgetting is very important. It allows us to free ourselves of resentments and marks of honour, of defilements and external burdens from our past, in order to keep only what is inscribed in the essence of our beings, through which we are what we are now. Thus unburdened, we can run forward, agile and unattached, straining with all our efforts towards our end, in a manner that leaves all attainments behind, without ever pausing in this life: 'Draw me after you, let us make haste' (Song of Songs 1:4). Christ is always ahead of us. Union with God comes to us as a perpetual novelty, a beginning ever renewed. Supported as we are by the ladder that links earth to heaven, which Jacob saw, God calls us to ascend to him. The ladder is Christ, and each rung always leads to another above it. We are constantly at the beginning with respect to what is above us.

The person who runs towards the Lord will never lack space for movement on his divine journey. For he must constantly raise himself and never stop drawing close as he runs to him who said: 'Rise up, and come' – and who at each moment gives the grace of a further ascent (Gregory of Nyssa).

This spiritual going beyond oneself is not a particular stage of the spiritual life: it is the actual condition of our existence. The spirit, as an immaterial and intelligible reality, is of itself unlimited; in this regard, God and the soul resemble each other.

> But God is the uncreated reality and the creator of all beings, who is always what he is . . . On the other hand, there is the reality brought into being by its creation, which is always orientated towards the first cause and is preserved in goodness by its participation in what enfolds it, to such an extent that in a certain sense, it is continually being created, growing by its increase in goodness, so that it no longer has a visible limit, nor can its increase in goodness and love be circumscribed by any boundary. (Gregory of Nyssa)

The created being can always become greater. If God is infinite in reality, the soul is infinite in potential. Its divinity consists in transforming itself into God. If it is infinite in potential, its creation must take the form of a process of growth, without which it would be simply finite in the way that the material world is. In this perspective, continual progress is constitutive of the soul itself; and it keeps itself constantly oriented towards something higher than itself.

There is something of fundamental importance here for our daily way of life.

Let us again try a little experiment. Close your eyes, breathe two or three times, deeply and slowly. Become aware of your body, then enter into yourself, to the very source of your being. Then, as you sit there calmly, visualize yourselves on the screen of your imagination. See your body irradiated by light. In this way, you are enfolded in the love of God, a love which gives you life both in your material existence – the breathing we receive expresses this well – and in your spiritual existence. Existence as a created spirit capable of unlimited growth in knowledge and love. Existence as the adopted children of God who plunges us into his own intimate life. This life is given to us at every moment in a relationship of grace and freedom which allows us to grow unceasingly in goodness and love even to the fullness of Christ which is without limit.

Let us become conscious of this light of love that surrounds

us. Love touches us through every object that we see, both
small and great, the mountain and the tree, the sun and the
candle. It sings in the song of birds, reveals itself in the murmur
of a brook. In Christ, but also in each brother we encounter,
it takes on a human face. It intervenes in our lives through all
the events which make our lives what they are. It is constantly
there in our heart, the presence of the Lord whose name punc-
tuates our breathing. We breathe the love which made us, here
and now.

Consciously, and with an abandonment that is utterly trusting, I open myself to this life and love which, in God, are
eternal: the creative action of God, in God, is God himself.
Only its consequences take place within time. Each present
moment links me with eternity, carries me in the Son towards
the Father in the love of the Spirit. That moment is enriched
by the past, and bears the future within itself in so far as I
surrender myself to it in faith. Forgetting the past, I strain
forward towards the goal, allowing myself to be carried by the
movement of the present.

It is precisely the reality of my present participation in the
life of God which, in fulfilling me, kindles my desire and orients
it towards its source. I orient myself by forgetting, by the poverty of my empty hands. I soar upwards by means of my desire.
Every moment is an absolute beginning. I receive myself utterly
anew, and give myself utterly without condition. The joy of my
gratitude, and my praise for the love and mercy of God which
enfold me, are together the song of my creation.

But what is obtained cannot become a limit to my desire. It
is not God. The most dazzling light, the most intense experience of love, the greatest possible revelation of his beauty – not
even these things are the One who is infinite, incomprehensible,
always beyond us. To find him, therefore, I must always go
higher in order to encounter his unending newness.

To reach the Creator, I must make myself a creator – at least
in so far as my dispositions are concerned. I must break all
the moulds in which I constantly fashion myself, for they are
invariably restrictive; I must reject all securities, all familiar
words, all riches, so as to offer myself utterly poor and virginal
to the breath of the Spirit. In this way is the only creativity that

counts made possible: the creativity that forms Christ in us, that gives birth to the Son; the creativity which forms ourselves, not just some object, into a poem of love to God, a poem that is completely unique.

Sometimes the Spirit gives me my being through solemn words of love, sometimes through words of joy. There are very mundane words, like bread, or water; there are words of humiliation, of suffering, even of sin. It is necessary to let ourselves be formed, through these various words, so that the glory of God may be sung.

If I am the poet of the poem which is my life, I am also the priest. The word which is given to me – as a Christian* and, in a particular way, as a priest – has the power to transform all things into the body of Christ. This is my body, this is my blood, given for you. Just as God creates, by his Word, at every moment, so he recreates us, takes us up again in all our humanity, with the whole of creation, into the eternal offering of the love of Christ to the Father, into the heart of which we are immersed by the sacrifice of the Mass.

Let us experience together a day of creation. Let us enter into ourselves, to where the source of our being springs forth. Every morning is a completely new beginning. God creates the heavens and the earth at this moment. I open my eyes on the morning of creation: I receive from the hands of God the gift of being, entirely new. Our first movement must be an outburst of wonder and gratitude. The sun rises. We must hasten to meet this love, which comes towards us in the tasks and events, however trivial, of our day. We need to pay attention to the discreet presence of the love which enfolds us, to its acts of tenderness that are often so personal. This creative attention, this trust and receptivity, are perhaps in themselves a very simple form of continual prayer. We need to receive the words of our poem in joy and abandonment to the Spirit who inspires them, whether or not they are what we want to hear. What do

---

* The priesthood of the faithful is a genuine participation in the priesthood of Christ, and gives us from the start the power of offering ourselves and all things in Christ, with the ordained priest. This dignity conferred in baptism is all too often forgotten.

we know? When the words exceed our understanding, when the melody is halting, unexpected, or full of half-tones, we break free from our limits and rise above ourselves. This melody and these words, so simple and yet concrete, are the hidden dwelling place of the Word: they bear within them the form of Christ; they say 'Father'.

> In the beginning was the Word,
> And the Word was with God,
> And the Word was God.
> He was in the beginning with God.
> All things came into being through him,
> And without him not one thing came into
>   being.
> What has come into being in him was life,
> And the life was the light of all people.
>   (John 1:1–4 NRSV)

Every morning, let us plunge our very being, and our day, into the river of love which flows from the Father to the Son through the Spirit, to return from the Son to the Father in a blaze of love. This is what creation is; this is what the Mass is. Let us welcome, consecrate and offer ourselves, our verse for today, in the eternal Eucharist, the hymn of thanksgiving to love. What is given us belongs to us no longer: our offering is the passage (the Passover) of our life into God. This happens by the dispossession of forgetfulness, in the remembrance of God alone. We turn, we move forward in faith and trust, towards him who comes and who will come.

Every Hour of the Office is a renewal of this consecration and this praise. This prayer is not a period of time shut off from our life, but the key point within it; for at every moment, in every object, person and event, God communicates himself; his Son is made flesh; the Spirit unites us with the hidden bonds of love.

'God saw everything that he made, and indeed, it was very good. And there was evening and there was morning' (Genesis 1).

In the evening, I give my being to the Father: I yield my life to him, I entrust myself to him in the repose of the seventh day. Every night I die in faith, possessing only my poverty and my trust, the peace of a hope which knows no calculation and seeks no assurance.

Is not the Father there, the Father whose love espies me, even though I am far away? He runs to throw himself on my neck and cover me with kisses. 'But Father, I have sinned!' 'Quickly, bring out the best robe . . . put a ring on his finger, and sandals on his feet.'

So let us go forth, flowers for a day, 'from beginnings to beginnings, through beginnings which never end' (Gregory of Nyssa).

Come, Lord Jesus!

25

Reborn Every Moment*

From the womb before the dawn I begot you.
(Psalm 110:3)

My dear friends,

After the more moving celebrations of Christmas and the Epiphany, the Presentation of our Lord may seem a rather less radiant mystery. The scene of Mary and Joseph bringing their little child to the Temple is more austere than the intimate joys of the Crib at Christmas, or the colourful adoration of the Magi. And yet the Presentation marks the summit of the mysteries of the infancy of Jesus. Up until now, men of good will were coming to offer him their homage. Today it is he himself who is being presented in the Temple. This little child, who is the Son of God, comes in his mother's arms to be in his Father's presence. It is a mystery of silence; and it is only twelve years later that Jesus will begin to reveal to us the depths of this mystery, when he speaks and tells us that his real home is there in the presence of his Father.

This mystery of the childhood of Christ must not only arouse in us a feeling of tenderness. It introduces us, in a very real way, to what Jesus will try to make us grasp all through his public life: he is the Son, and he comes to invite us to share in his eternal birth. On this day of your entry into the community, I suggest that we meditate on this theme. Monastic life requires us to undergo a conversion. This conversion is a new birth in

---

*Sermon preached on the Feast of the Presentation of our Lord, for the Clothing of two Brothers.

Jesus, and with him. In practical terms, how are we to go about this complete change in our whole life that is required of us?

The message of the Gospel is first of all a call to conversion. John the Baptist and Jesus himself and the Apostles after him all continually repeat this call: 'Be converted'. Monastic life is firmly set in the same direction. In the Western monastic tradition, there is a vow of conversion of life: that is, the obligation of continual conversion, of never giving up on this effort to transform ourselves in order to become more conformed to what God wants of us. That is why there is a chapter on conversion of life in our Statutes. The new habit that you are soon to don is the visible symbol of this continual interior transformation to which you are now committed. But what does this conversion consist in?

It is always risky to try to resume in a few words the teaching of Jesus on this subject. But I don't think we will be unfaithful to this teaching if we give priority to the uncompromising phrase he used, to the astonishment of his disciples: 'Unless you are converted, unless you change yourselves and become like little children, you will never enter the kingdom of heaven' (Matthew 18:3). This idea runs through the whole Gospel, but it is something we have difficulty in assimilating, since it goes so much against everything in us that desires to be great and strong and is determined to become 'adult'. However, Jesus does not compromise. In his conversation with Nicodemus, he goes to the bottom of the question: 'Unless one is born anew, he cannot see the kingdom of God' (John 3:3). And when Nicodemus protests, Jesus only repeats all the more strongly what he has already affirmed. So this is the conversion that is required of us: we must become capable of being reborn. We cannot help wondering, like Nicodemus: 'Do we have to return into our mother's womb?' For us, becoming a child again is associated with childishness and all sorts of amusing attitudes, and we cannot believe that is what God wants of us. That is not the example that Jesus left us. If we want to understand the meaning of the conversion to which he is calling us, he is the one we must contemplate: Jesus himself is the source of the transformation he asks of us.

Several times in the Statutes we are told that our ideal is Jesus living in dependence on his Father. Throughout the Gospel, our Lord gives us intimations of this mystery: he speaks of his desire to do the will of the Father; in his teaching, he is only repeating what he hears from his Father; his works have their source in the Father, etc. All this is a pointer for us, but leaves us with a deeper mystery: the mystery of Jesus in the presence of his Father. The exterior actions of our Lord, however rich in teaching they may be, are meant to introduce us into the interior movement by which he is turned towards his Father, where he no longer has anything to say to others, or any exterior actions to accomplish, but where his inner being is simply in the presence of the One who gives him birth. 'Today I have begotten you,' we often repeat when singing the psalms. The Father engenders the Son; Jesus, the human face of the Father, in turn engenders us.

This is the conversion that is required of us: we are to renounce living as autonomous, self-sufficient beings who stand before God and man with a certain self-confidence, as though we had something in ourselves that we had not received. A little child is not only weak, charming and fragile, but above all, someone who receives life from another. Being a son of man not only means receiving material existence from one's father, a body formed during many months in a mother's womb; above all, it means receiving one's being as a person, capable of perceiving the love in the eyes of the father leaning over him, the gaze of a father who sees in his son an absolutely unique being, another himself. On a human level, this reality is always lived in a very imperfect, fragmentary way and fraught with difficulties. But it is an analogy of the infinitely more beautiful and certain reality that we must try to live with our heavenly Father, who reveals himself to us in his Son. It is here that we can see at last the full realization of the call that resounds through the whole of the Old Testament, as a leitmotif: that the light of God's face should shine upon us, and that this light should be a source of life for us.

On a level that we can barely grasp, there is a fundamental difference between human paternity as we know it and the paternity of God which is revealed in secret. For a human child, growing up and becoming himself implies a certain breaking away from his father and freeing himself from a state of dependency which is burdensome if it lasts too long, since, by its nature, it is only temporary. But for the child of God, on the contrary, being born is not something that happens once and for all at some particular moment in time, after which he must gradually learn to fly with his own wings: it means receiving from God at every single moment the divine life that makes us his children. It means remaining in the attitude of one who is repeatedly beginning again, opening ourselves continually, as if for the very first time, to the loving gaze of God which gives us our existence. It is this mystery of childhood that is revealed to us in the Presentation of our Lord: Jesus shows himself to us as being the Child *par excellence*. He was born of Mary and in today's feast, we begin to see how, in his whole being, he is dependent on the love he receives from the Father. This is the state that is the goal of our own conversion.

We would obviously need to dwell much longer on this in order to show how these Gospel truths are fulfilled in the monastic life. Let us simply consider a few aspects that you will later be able to reflect on, and, more importantly, to live.

If you are here today asking to receive the monastic habit, it is because the light of God's face has already shone upon you and seduced you. That is what is at the heart of the monastic conversion, to which you are committing yourself. Even if there are times of darkness to come, this initial calling will remain, ever true and effective: God has invited you to become his children in all truth, to be nothing else but his sons, to be uniquely those who live in the light of his face. The solid foundation of your monastic life is that God has called you: God, to whom you know every step will lead you, in spite of all the twists and turns that circumstances, your own poverty, and perhaps your faults, may seem to impose upon you.

But you will have to respond to the Father's call with an effort of personal asceticism. In order to be born again, you will have to lose the 'persona' you had in your eyes and that you tried to play out before others. That is the fundamental asceticism: to be freed from oneself, to do away with the complex and sturdy scaffolding that we have constructed in order to rely on our own strength and count on our own reserves,

VERY
IMPORTANT

and have the impression that all the guarantees we need are within our own selves. One day all that must fall to pieces, so that we can come before the Father as children who have no other protection than his loving care. Try then to do away with all avarice and possessiveness, every attachment to what you think is yours. Your only treasure is the gift God is making you of his own self, and which enables you to be yourselves, not so much in the eyes of men, but in the eyes of the Father, the Son and the Holy Spirit.

At this point, it is a whole commentary on the Statutes that we would have to undertake. We would see how all our observances converge in order to free us to listen to the Lord and let him penetrate within us and make us receptive to his word; in short, they exist in order to open us up completely, so that the Father, who wants to communicate himself to us in his Son, can invade and overwhelm us. Solitude, silence, poverty, the liturgy and the various austerities are all different facets of one and the same movement: by these exterior means, in the charity of community life and the unity of one body, we are to become sons of the Father, in Jesus.

We cannot end these reflections without mentioning the role of our Lady. She has been present in all that we have said, for there can be no child without a mother; here below, there can be no birth without a heart that has received, even before the child, the love descending from the Father. So it is in dependence on Mary, and enveloped in her tenderness and receptivity, that we can learn how to be converted, that is, how to be born, how to be simply God's children. 'Jesus was born of woman . . . so that we might receive adoption as sons,' says St Paul (Galatians 4:5). Let us then entrust ourselves to her who is blessed among women, and she will teach us how to say in the Spirit: 'Abba, Father'. Amen.

POVERTY

26

Towards a Divine Poverty

> Everything that is mine is yours,
> just as that which is yours is mine.
> **(John 17:10)**

Dear Fathers and Brothers,

Each year we are invited during Lent to journey yet further into the desert with Jesus. That invitation calls for no important change in the outward pattern of our lives, but is an inward call to us by the Spirit to better discover the meaning of solitude and, therefore, of the total poverty which it implies. For every Christian, since the Beatitudes, poverty is the first key to the Kingdom, the condition by which he achieves intimacy with Jesus; for it is in tune with the fundamental attitude of Jesus' heart. Do we not, rather, have a tendency to think of poverty in a negative way as a deprivation? In particular, instead of considering poverty as influencing our relations with others, does it not risk shutting us up in a narrow world of our own? Let us now try, therefore, to examine poverty from the point of view of greater transparency in our relations with others and with God.

Let us begin with a sort of examination of conscience. Just think of all the lack of genuine poverty so evident in our attitude towards our brothers, and even in our attitude towards the Lord. These may seem at first sight to have nothing to do with poverty; but we will not have to dig too deeply before we notice that they reveal a need in us to acquire something for ourselves, to possess something not our own. For example, consider the extraordinary ease with which we judge and condemn our brothers. As soon as their behaviour does not conform to our desires, we are taken aback and quickly drawn to find fault. We make some critical remark in a few cutting words. Spontaneously, we set ourselves up as their judges, having decided that we have the right to condemn them, to put ourselves above them, to judge what are their innermost thoughts. We were afraid to make the effort to understand, which doubtless would have allowed us to enter into their perspectives, perhaps to admit that they were right, or at least to sympathize with their weaknesses, in the experience that we have of our own poverty. It is a type of instinctive self-defence, a misguided search for security. It seems that our inner equilibrium is called into question when our brother does not behave as we do. We feel unable to share with him what is most personal to us.

Let us continue this little inquiry by recalling in how many ways we are subject to our hypersensitivity. It is a well-known temptation of the solitary to imagine himself the object of unfavourable judgements, to believe that not enough consideration is shown him, to be hurt for no reason. We must not take the easy way out and excuse ourselves by thinking: since solitude necessarily makes us susceptible, let us simply accept this kind of reaction every time we are contradicted. In reality, this hypersensitivity is a permanent sore which taints a part of our solitude. It shows that our life in the desert is a life lived only with ourselves. We can no longer allow others to enter into our life; at least in our heart and feelings, the ability truly to welcome our brothers and sisters gradually disappears. We judge everything in relation to our personal reactions; we are unable to see objectively what is obvious to everyone else. Are we not then as far from poverty as possible? As soon as anyone interferes with our little treasures, we are cut to the quick. Is not this the sign of a possessive spirit with respect to ourselves? It is a painful experience, but each one of us should be honest enough to examine himself, without thinking that the cause lies above all with his neighbour.

Now that we have spoken about our relations with others,

let us move on to our relationship with the Lord. Do we not have a spontaneous tendency to present ourselves before him as though we had certain rights, obliging his goodness, as it were, to grace? We do not like to remain destitute, in dryness and darkness, and esteem that we have done all that was necessary to be duly entitled to a reward. Basically, without daring to say so, we rely on our own merits, our holiness and virtues. Undoubtedly we would not dare to say so explicitly, but in reality we react thus: whether we become disheartened, disillusioned or impatient with the Lord's delays, the underlying sentiment is the same: how is it that things don't go better, seeing that I've done everything required to achieve good results? In dealing with the love of God, we think we have some sort of exchange currency; we imagine that we are rich, whereas our only title-deed in his eyes is our poverty.

There is no point in prolonging this examination of conscience. Rather let us ask ourselves how it is that we manage to pervert what is best in our life: fraternal love, solitude, intimacy with God. These are the purest elements of our calling and our reactions tend precisely to strip them of their purity, continually distorting them by our spiritual possessiveness. How is it possible that in the midst of a lifestyle in which asceticism and purification so predominate, we still remain such prisoners of ourselves? Is it not because there is something wrong in the way we conceive of asceticism and the effort of renunciation asked of us by Christ in the Gospel? He speaks to us of a burden that is light and a yoke that is easy; yet the reactions of which we have been speaking are rather redolent of a bitterness in our hearts, a sort of defence against a load too heavy to bear. Are we not victims of a too negative, almost destructive, idea of asceticism? Are we not unconsciously cloaking ourselves in a ludicrous counterfeit asceticism instead of giving what the Lords asks of us?

The asceticism that ought to free us from ourselves ends up instead by turning us in on ourselves, cutting off all communication. Is that not because we somehow conceive of our efforts of purification as a sort of mutilation of our innermost self, a violence done by the will to the rest of our nature? Asceticism ends by becoming cold and inhuman, something we put up with because we cannot do otherwise, which crushes us instead of expanding our hearts. So let us try to look for a few moments of the real nature of solitude and poverty with new eyes and a more transparent gaze.

What is the desert in the eyes of God? The prophets, when they speak of the time of the Exodus, or when they envisage the return of the exiles to Jerusalem, think of the wilderness first and foremost as a place of tenderness and intimacy. The wilderness is the privileged setting into which God, in his boundless love, draws the one he cherishes in order to give himself to him. It is the whole mystery of Israel in the desert which is thus summed up in the tenderness of God, who seeks to free his friend from all shackles, so that they might meet in a secluded place, far from misleading distractions, in intimacy of heart.

It is from the same viewpoint that we should consider poverty. This is the very first condition of a mutual gift, of a love in which we stake our very selves and not all those goods which are exterior to ourselves. To be poor is to have acquired complete freedom to give of oneself and receive. Here again, let us remember the continual summons of God in the Old Testament: he asks his people not to rely on their own strength, nor to rely on human friends, nor to think that when they possess material wealth that this provides them with security; God has but one goal: to convince his people that their one and only support is himself, Yahweh, the living God, full of tenderness and mercy.

It is this which Jesus shows us in a concrete way in his own life, that he is nothing but receptivity to his Father. It is that which he shows us also in Mary, from the Annunciation to Calvary. Total poverty is not a ruthless stripping according to rigid requirements, but the deeper and more exacting renunciation that is total availability, a boundless flexibility that allows us to respond to everything that the Lord asks of us through his spirit or through a human intermediary. The face of poverty bears the features of love and not those of the cross.

There is nothing particularly new in what we have said so far. So, why do we have such difficulty in seeing things as they really are? Might it not be that the image of God which we have is distorted? Do we see sufficiently in him the deep, living and luminous source of a poverty which is joy and the gift of self? If we perceived this loving and attentive attitude on the part of the Father who gives himself to us through all our deprivations, we would attain poverty without effort and not display those symptoms of turning in on ourselves of which we spoke above. We should therefore direct our humble and fascinated gaze towards the mystery of a God in whom everything is total poverty because everything there is love; for it is by this 'poverty-love' that we live.

Jesus repeats to us unceasingly: the Father loves the Son and gives him both everything he has and, above all, everything he is. The Father keeps nothing for himself. He makes no reservation, and holds nothing back. The Son is his perfect image because the Father has withheld nothing and given everything to the Son. In the Father we find the infinite poverty of giving. This poverty is shown above all by the fact that the Father imposes absolutely nothing on his Son. He allows him to be himself. Once it appears in the Son, the Father's gift is but the Son: the Father has effaced himself to allow his Child to be himself. The Father begets the Son in complete respect and freedom.

The Son, for his part, possesses nothing which comes from himself. All that he has is completely received; everything comes from the Father's hands. In the Son we find the infinite poverty of receiving. His joy is in knowing that he cannot rely on himself, but he receives everything from the limitless generosity of his Father. The Son is such a perfect image of the Father that he is likewise incapable of keeping anything for himself. It is impossible for him to turn in on himself or to enjoy possessing anything whatsoever: as the image of an infinite gift he is himself infinite gift, and in order to give the Father complete joy, he makes a total return to him of all that he is. To this limitless poverty of giving on the part of the Father, and to the limitless poverty of the Son's receiving this gift, corresponds the boundless poverty of transparency on the part of the Spirit. He is able neither to give nor to receive. He is simple communication, receiving everything from the Father and the Son simultaneously, without holding on to anything. He is neither source nor receptivity. He is simply transparency and the possibility for the other two Persons to encounter each other fully. What the Father and the Son have in common is nothing of themselves, but a third Person whose being is perfect and complete in himself just as theirs is.

Human words can scarcely scratch the surface of this mystery of love which is at the same time a mystery of poverty. Yet, such is the model which should inspire our attitude as monks. We are invited by the generosity of the Father to enter into this movement of unlimited giving and receiving, bathed in the light of divine transparency. Such is the true meaning of poverty: not an annoyance, not a mere deprivation, but an opening out which enables us to become perfectly ourselves by accepting to have nothing for ourselves.

It is time to bring these reflections to a close. They call for a practical response on our part. This should not be a reflex toward greater and more rigid austerity in the face of the faults to which we referred at the beginning, but rather a reaction of true poverty, a healthy poverty, aware of how much we are closed in on ourselves, greedy and egotistical. May these miseries that we notice in ourselves be only a more pressing invitation to turn ourselves towards the love of the Father so that the Son may be born in us in the limpid transparency of the Spirit. Thus, at one and the same time, will we finally become perfectly ourselves and give ourselves perfectly to God. May the Virgin Mary, whose simplicity summed up in itself the receptivity of the entire human race, obtain this grace for us.

27

Contemplative Poverty

Contemplation is a participation in divine life, in the knowledge and love of God. Christian contemplation is the awakening of the life of Christ in us through the breath of the Spirit: his gaze on the Father, his love for mankind. Our prayer is a bringing to the fore of the grace of Christ by which, as members of Christ's body, sons in the Son, we enter into the life of the Trinity: the exchange of love among the Father, the Son and the Holy Spirit.

The Father is the source of everything; through love he gives everything to the Son. His joy is in giving, in giving his very self: total fruitfulness, eternal poverty, because he keeps nothing back for himself. The Father sends himself forth totally in his unique Word.

The Son receives everything from the Father, eternally. To be the Son is always to be turned towards the Father so as to receive everything from him, and by the power of this received life, to give everything back to the Father in a rebounding of love and gratitude.

This outpouring, the link which unites the Father and the Son in a reciprocal gift of love, is the Holy Spirit, poverty twice over: born of the gift, in the gift, for the gift. Divine love only exists as giving itself, as losing itself completely and eternally.

Since God is love, the life of the Trinity is seen as the unconditional gift of reciprocal love. In the Three Persons, the divine nature exists precisely as given. Who can be poorer than God? He alone knows how to give himself completely. And precisely by this 'Gift-Love', he is fulfilled. This law is seen to be verified in the incarnation of the Son:

His state was divine,
Yet he did not cling
to this equality with God
but emptied himself
to assume the condition of a slave . . .
he was humbler yet,
even to accepting death,
death on a cross.

(Philippians 2:6–8 JB)

God has filled with his glory the one who emptied himself, and with the Father, the Son becomes a source for us of the gift of the Spirit. In order to receive the gift of God we must follow the example of Christ in his poverty: to turn all our desire towards the Father, to be complete receptivity, welcoming readiness. In order that this may be possible, we must purify our desire of anything that has an undue hold over it, from the many things we covet and from superficial gratifications; we must be poor in spirit with a heart that is poor, free, young and unencumbered.

The gift of God, grace, is a unique and indivisible reality, a participation in divine life, which can only be differentiated by the three powers of the soul. Faith is the transferring of all criteria of truth, from the 'I' who understands to the eternal 'Thou'. Hope is the renouncing of the benefits and causes of all human consolation so as to remain solely in expectation of God himself. Charity is the gift of all our being to the beloved God.

This poverty encompasses everything: the material, intellectual, affective and spiritual.

MATERIAL POVERTY

This is a firm renunciation of the possession of material goods, and the simple use without attachment of the necessities that obedience (itself a dispossession of our own will) puts at our disposal. It means being a pilgrim on earth, *en route* to our homeland, without becoming installed in a place, in a job, or in any kind of security. There is a certain tension between the monastic stability which normally binds us to a house, and the non-attachment required (or called for) by poverty. It seems to be that the second takes precedence over the first; for example, if we are asked to go to another house because of the needs of that house, ordinarily we ought to show ourselves willing. It is evangelical unconcern: no worrying about yesterday, today or tomorrow, and confidence in Divine Providence which governs everything with wisdom and measure. The Father will give to the Order, the House and each one of us our daily bread, if we know how to ask for it with humility. None of this means that we are exempt from the law of work: rather, the poor man accepts as his lot a hard and thankless workload. He is exposed to the vicissitudes of the seasons. His time is not his own; let him give it without stint to whoever asks it of him; as also his attention and affection.

INTELLECTUAL POVERTY

Watertight formulas come readily to the pen: night, cloud of unknowing, rejection of all clear knowledge so as to plunge oneself into what is ineffable, etc. These formulas are true, but only in their context.

I would like to dwell here on our everyday lives, on what is accessible to us each day. The liturgy, reading, meditation, work, simply remaining in the presence of God, prayer: all these things are woven together from words and images, from symbols and from silence.

Our communion with God and with our brothers is realized concretely in this way, but the proportion of these elements will be different for different people and even for a single person, according to the evolution of his or her spiritual life. The mediation of ideas and images can be more or less pronounced or necessary according to the particular case, without necessarily being a criterion of the spiritual level attained: graces, like temperaments, differ.

That being said, one can speak of a way by signs and of a way beyond signs. Let it be said straightaway that the way beyond signs cannot exist without a preliminary and accompanying passage through the way of signs. The point of departure is the knowledge of things given by God through signs (nature, experience of the senses, the revealed Word, Christ), and the spiritual journey relies on these signs and on their extensions in the sacraments, the liturgy, our brothers, art, etc. Christ always remains the Way. The way which goes from the tangible and clear to the spiritual conforms to the nature of man, embodied spirit, and to the Christian dogma: God created everything good. He is immanent in everything that has being. Christ gathers together all that is tangible so as to place it, in union with himself, in the life of the Trinity.

Man is a complex being. His vital energy, made up as it is of emotion and passion, expressing his basic instincts, needs the direction of reason informed by faith. We cannot give ourselves up with impunity to the dark and anarchic forces which lie deep within us. At the same time, there is no need to box ourselves into a narrow rationalism which reduces reality to what can be manipulated and controlled by logical concepts, and inserted into the interior world which we have made for ourselves. Such knowledge easily becomes possession, object of a grasping ego and an exaltation of ourselves. Reality is forced into a narrow system and reduced to our own personal standard. It is imperative therefore to remain open to a 'true reality' which is not our own construct and to revere its mystery. This is done in two ways: by humble and genuine contact with the world of the senses in all its density and beauty; by openness to values beyond ourselves, to other people and to God. This knowledge is born in the depths of the heart, which, curiously, communicate most directly with the subconscious. Reason informed by faith maintains its prerogative of discernment: it does not itself give life, but is a help in unmasking life's counterfeits.

There is no other religion besides Christianity which puts forward so many dogmas and which formulates them with such intellectual precision; at the same time, in no other religion are there so many mysteries which so completely surpass reason. But once we have reached the limits of what is tangible and intelligible, love sometimes plunges into a beyond which is absolute mystery, that is, God in his transcendence. Here is a way beyond signs, which one enters only in response to a call from the Lord.

Between the sign and the mystery, there is a rupture which is death, or darkness (call it what you will). It is the way of non-feeling and unknowing.

Faith is an infused virtue, a fountain springing up within us, something of God himself, of his own pure light. If one wishes to see and find assurance in the domain of the finite, he only disturbs this obscure light which opens onto the infinity of God. In fact, it is in blinding our limited understanding that faith imbues it with this light.

Our habitual gaze on God gradually becomes concentrated in a single act, very pure and generalized, which brings about a loving knowledge, general and indistinct, a light that is spiritual and simple and neither affected nor focused by any particular intelligible.

The obscure and unfocused nature of this knowledge is, for the beginner, an experience of complete darkness: a radical deprivation of normal understanding, stripping of natural light which nonetheless makes possible the passage to an interior resurrection of the spirit, the awakening of the divine life in us, and a different way of knowing, loving and being in God.

This way is high and dangerous. We must stay in the realm of signs and symbols so long as we are not constrained to leave it for the paths of the Spirit. It is not that forms are rejected, the perceptible signs of the mystery; in fact, we are being deprived of them, and only temporarily. If by pride and brashness we launch into the realm prematurely, we risk the worst possible spiritual and even psychological deviations. Humility alone can save us from that.

Nearly all those who turn towards the Carthusian life feel a secret call to silence, to the mystery that is still unknown, yet somehow already loved. Solitude will purge us from presumption and illusion. Little by little, the light of eternity in which we are continually bathed will put everything in its rightful place in the order of things. Silence will develop and become filled with humble adoration.

In the end, our intellectual poverty is to renounce all rational 'possession' of God (in other words to renounce all the idols which we have made in our image and to our own measure) in order to be pure receptivity to the Mystery that he will forever remain, even while giving himself completely to us as he is. Communion with this Mystery really does exist.

The darkness nurtures a hidden fire which, otherwise, would swallow it up. Loving faith rediscovers signs, but in a different manner; its purified gaze makes signs transparent to God, to the world of revealed truth, to the humanity of Christ: while remaining exactly what they are, they nonetheless become like clear crystal through which the divine light passes unobstructed. A tree is a tree, bread is bread, wind is wind; but in another dimension, on another level of consciousness, all is light, all is God. For God is not an object among other objects. It is for this reason that our understanding, made to know material things, only knows him as darkness.

In order to know God, we must become as he is and be introduced to a way of knowing, God's way, which is no different from his very being. This knowledge is transformation, love, Spirit.

> You must give up our old way of life; you must put aside your old self, which gets corrupted by following illusory desires. Your mind must be renewed by a spiritual revolution so that you can put on the new self that has been created in God's way, in the goodness and the holiness of the truth. (Ephesians 4:22–24 JB)

POVERTY OF THE AFFECTIONS

I only skim the surface of this aspect of our poverty, since we shall deal with it in greater depth in relation to the vow of chastity. It is very real, however, and sometimes the young monk will acutely feel the absence of his relatives and friends. The brothers given him by the Lord will often not be as close to him as those bound to him by blood or by the same social milieu. Time is necessary to forge new bonds in the Spirit. It will happen, though, with the help of grace.

SPIRITUAL POVERTY

Spiritual poverty is placed between the act of receiving all and our desire to give all.

God's love for us is purely gratuitous. Everything we have, absolutely everything, has been given to us. The only thing that comes from us is the evil we do. We have no right to be proud of anything, unless in the Lord. If we have received some natural or supernatural gift, we are only its trustees; this gift is destined for the good of all and we will have to answer for it before the Lord.

But it is more subtle and difficult to avoid selfishness and greed with respect to spiritual blessings. The young monk becomes puffed up with the lights and consolations that the Lord gives him, not realizing that it is but milk for the child he is. Such is his pleasure that he applies himself to his spiritual exercises with an obvious gluttony, sometimes to the detriment of his readiness to carry out his duties in the community.

He places himself above others whom he judges less favoured, and thus less holy, than he. He judges them with pride, even with scorn. He ascribes to himself the gifts of God, believing himself rich, while he is far from the Lord.

He reads the experiences of the great mystics and finds described there, or so he thinks, his own experiences. Yet, for the most part, he has not even crossed the threshold of supernatural prayer, except, perhaps, at certain odd moments which do not correspond to his habitual level. He does not know that there is a certain similarity between the pattern of the first steps in the life of prayer and the highest degrees, but that the latter are at an infinitely superior level. There are few novices who do not fall, more or less, into this trap. The unmistakeable symptom is pride. A human being before the true God is always profoundly humble and forgetful of self.

It is only slowly that the necessary process of purification is accomplished through God's action: alternating consolations and dryness lead to an authentic faith; deepening knowledge of ourselves is joined to an ever deeper knowledge of the merciful love of God, without which this knowledge would be unbearable; providential trials make us all the more aware of our weakness. At last, we come to understand that we are nothing, but that God loves us in spite of everything; that he became man in order to enter into communion with us, that grace works in us and through us; grace is everything.

We have no right to claim as our own the good which we do. We do not even have the absolute certainty of believing in God, of loving him or our brothers. Each morning we must receive everything anew in faith. God creates us truly at every moment. The past, we entrust to his mercy; we must empty our memory of its supposed riches so as to change it into a pure movement toward God himself beyond his gifts. This movement is lived uniquely in the reality of the present moment, in our conforming to the will of the Lord for us, here and now, in our communion of love and our close attention to him. Here poverty and simplicity become one. For the future, we entrust ourselves to God. We do not, as it were, have an account in some celestial bank; all we have is our faith in the love of the Lord, our hope and our desire to love.

We must not be anxious before the demands of true spiritual poverty. We are never so well off as when we have nothing. We are free and available for anything. Our ego, weak as it is, would like to cover its nakedness with furs made of material things, and intellectual and spiritual goods. The obscure light of faith is a light indeed, and whoever becomes accustomed to it will not abandon it for all the sweetness and consolations of days gone by. May God preserve us from our virtues! Our faith allows us to discard this deceitful covering in order to walk in truth along the path which is no path, which leads to the Father in Love, that is, in the Spirit of Christ. The man who is poor finds the gates of death open, and he passes freely into the Kingdom of God. For if we despoil ourselves, it is in order to rediscover the innocent nakedness of God's image in our hearts and thus to clothe ourselves in Christ (Galatians 4:27). Our poverty is the poverty of the children of God, who 'having nothing, yet possess all' (2 Corinthians 6:10) in hope and in faith. We have received 'a spirit of adoption as sons, by virtue of which we cry, "Abba! Father!" ' (Romans 8:15–17).

IMAGES OF CONTEMPLATIVE POVERTY

Severe elegance of the essential. A stone sculpture.

Silhouette of roofs under a starry sky.

Not to pick the flowers.

To love the rose for itself.

Shunning honours, special graces, success.

Indifference to the results of particular actions.

Equanimity in joy and suffering.

Absolute respect for one's fellow man.

To rejoice in the riches of others as if they were our own. (This one is very difficult.)

To accept oneself with one's limitations and failings.

To accept being little known, unknown, misjudged or despised by men if that should happen.

The hidden name.

To know how to hope in God alone.

Mountain summit, eroded and bare, exposed rock.

To live the poverty of true love, the joy of need, the humility of giving oneself.

To let each moment of my time flow like sand between my fingers; not to hold it back from those who ask it of me.

To ask for nothing, to refuse nothing.

To accept constraint, within me and towards me.

Yes, Lord.

A leaf swept away by the breath of the Spirit.

Autumn leaf.

Ephemeral snowflake, lit up by the sun.

The limpid light of winter.

Sound of cow bells in the meadow.

Mountains forming a cup so as to catch at their rim the slanting light of autumn.

Chalice, sacrifice of praise.

To be receptive to all that exists.

To suffer; one's naked existence.

To let oneself breathe along with life itself,

Body calm, eyes closed, spirit vigilant.

A skiff on the sea.

OBEDIENCE

28

The Liberty of St Bruno*

I contemplate the splendour
of God's goodness towards you.
(St Bruno to his sons at the Charterhouse)

Dear Brothers,

We are deeply moved by St Bruno's Magnificat, when he
addresses the first lay brothers of the Grande Chartreuse. His
joy is overflowing, not because he sees them performing
miracles, or lost in ecstasy, but because they have discovered
the secret of true obedience. Spontaneously, Bruno echoes the
words of the Virgin Mary singing her joy to God, as he marvels
that 'the finger of Almighty God has engraved in the heart of
his sons not only the love, but also the knowledge of his holy
law' (id.). Overjoyed at discovering this, Bruno outlines a
description of obedience which, although brief, is so rich that
we can constantly return to it.

So let us listen to St Bruno, and, from the start, enter into his
perspectives. Here, he is not teaching us as a theologian, but
sharing with us a secret of his heart. The lay brothers he is
addressing have no academic learning, but they have allowed
Almighty God himself to teach them his ways of love and
knowledge. In the simplicity of their hearts, and moved by the
Holy Spirit, they gather the succulent and life-giving fruits
of Holy Scripture. We must try to have the same simplicity of

*Sermon preached on the Feast of St Bruno.

heart, as we too listen to St Bruno revealing to us something of the secret of obedience.

For him, obedience is at the heart of the contemplative life. It is 'the key and the seal of all our spiritual effort'. Everything is built upon obedience, and even at the summit of this edifice, we find obedience again. For our Father, it is not merely one virtue among others. For him, all the deepest realities of a life genuinely given to the Lord, humility and patience, love of the Lord and charity towards the brothers, have their point of convergence, as it were, in obedience. It is the unequivocal sign of the action of God in the soul of his beloved brothers; seeing the way they practise obedience, we have immediate access to the depths of their souls, to the light they have received from the Lord, and to the love that has been kindled there.

This requires us to examine our own conscience. It is so easy to flee from the reality of obedience, contenting ourselves with fine theories about it. It is so easy to evade it, claiming the right to affirm our personality on the grounds, we say, that we have received it from the Lord. In reality, when we are honest with ourselves, we cannot but admit that obedience is not easy. There is a great risk of forgetting this, especially for us solitaries. Left to ourselves, and living in the sight of God alone, his light should be our sole guide; but often, the absence of friendly feedback from our brothers or from those on whom we depend, leaves us drifting at the mercy of self-will.

Why is it that we do not manage to attain to the beautiful transparency with regard to God that Bruno's first companions had? We would then be ready for the finger of God to engrave all the secrets of his holy law in our own hearts as well. Is it not because we turn obedience into something complicated, even repulsive perhaps, instead of looking at Jesus in order to learn the meaning of it? How often the Gospel invites us to do this; the new Statutes, also, seem instinctively to link our obedience to that of the Saviour. So let us learn at the school of Jesus.

With extreme discretion, but in an infinitely profound way, the Gospels, particularly St John, allow us to enter into the intimate relationship which exists between the Father and Son. We can sense a link of dependency that is practically unlimited. Jesus does nothing of himself, but only what he has seen his Father doing. He does not decide anything, for everything comes from the Father. His only real food is to do the will of his Father. And, remarkably, such total dependency does not seem to be a burden to him. There is absolutely nothing to indicate that his constant concern with the Father's will makes him feel that he is prevented from living life to the full. On the contrary: this is the source of all his joy, all his serenity, and of the unfailing strength which allows him to face up to every situation with equanimity, in spite of so many adversities.

For the Lord, obedience is not a constraint which goes against his very nature. On the contrary, for him, obedience is returning to the roots of his being, as a child of God; it is drawing from the source of life: being the Son of the Father, and being the one whose obedience is perfect, are, for him, identical.

This is the model of obedience that is proposed to us. It is not a matter of learned debate, to decide if a particular rule applies to us today, or a question of calculating meticulously whether the Father has the right to ask this or that of us. There is nothing theoretical about the obedience of Jesus. It is quite simply a relationship of trust in someone. To obey means to turn our heart in trust towards the heart of another who loves us. This does not in any way contradict the great theological principles concerning the eternal laws of God. They are not contradicted, but presented in a form which is both more realistic and more convincing: we are the children of God, and it is this divine filiation that we must continually develop.

Our Statutes lead us in the same direction. We read 'The Prior does not judge according to human standards, but, together with his monks, strives to listen to the Spirit in a common seeking of the will of God' (23.4). What does listening to the Spirit mean? It means remaining attentively and trustingly in the presence of the One who, at this very moment in his goodness, is giving us life. We marvel at the intimate relationship between Jesus and his Father. Are we not invited to a similar relationship, in faith? The Lord's love for us is not an abstraction, or a beautiful idea to be set aside when dealing with the practicalities of life. No: it is a living reality which alone gives to every moment of our existence its true, profound meaning.

This is real obedience: seeking the unique truth to which Jesus bears witness, and which, he told us, was the reason for his coming. What is the truth of the heart of God, here and now, for me? This, quite simply, is what obedience is all about: in simplicity of heart, letting oneself be taught by the One who has promised to be always faithfully at our side.

Let us do our best to act in the light, and to come to the light, as Jesus invites us to do; it is in this light that we will be able to see, and be made capable of carrying out what we have seen. Let us be careful not to separate our life of prayer from our life of obedience: as St Bruno has shown us, they are one. If sometimes our soul is filled with all the bitterness of pseudo-obedience, it is because we have tried to escape from the relationship of trust and love that should always be there in our heart, with regard to God. There is never any need for us to defend our liberty against him, or to build ramparts around ourselves to guarantee our autonomy. On the contrary, it is God who is the only true source of this liberty, which enables us to love both him and our brothers.

But let us not delude ourselves. As we try to identify true obedience, our reflections are full of serenity and light; but this must not make us forget that, for Jesus, the ultimate accomplishment of the Father's will took the form of an infinitely painful testing.

The Letter to the Hebrews tells us this in unforgettable words: 'Although he was a Son, he learned obedience through what he suffered. And he was thus made perfect' (Hebrews 5:8–9).

We are always perplexed by this affirmation of the Scriptures: the Son of God needed to learn obedience. How much more then, do we ourselves need to develop it in our hearts! Obedience is not a static attitude; to be alive, it must grow continually, and daily progress in an understanding of its real nature as it comes up against all the occasions in which the will of God meets with our resistance.

Jesus, then, was put to the test, a test of his total fidelity to the will of the Father. We can compare the testing of Jesus to that of Adam. In both cases, what was required was a radical, essential obedience. It was a testing, not necessarily in the sense of a temptation from the devil, whispering his perfidious insinuations into the ear, though this may often be the case. It was, above all, another kind of testing: before granting the plenitude of divine filiation to his creature, God was asking to what extent he was prepared to receive everything from him, whatever the cost. For Jesus, in his human heart and intelligence, obedience was a testing of his absolute trust in the Father, who seemed to have totally abandoned him. And that is how he learned true obedience: by accepting the will of the Father who seemed to be deserting him.

It was also a part of his testing that Jesus should have to endure evil, sin and suffering on Calvary. It was the Father's will that the evil hidden in the heart of humanity should become the means by which His Son would restore all things. Jesus' obedience, and the close adhesion of his heart to the heart of the Father, led him to surrender himself without defence to all the effects of sin.

And it was thus that, one morning, he emerged into the great and eternal light of the Resurrection.

Is this not what is sometimes asked of us: to accept the will of God that disconcerts us completely? It seems to be separating us from God; it seems to be delivering us over to sin, or at least to error and ignorance. God wants to put us also to the test, so that we may learn true obedience, and become perfect in the image of his Son.

When this happens, it is no longer a time for reasoning, or arguing, or wanting to understand. More than ever, we have to believe in the love of God; in the depths of our heart, we must be born to a deeper trust in him, which in the end, is also a resurrection.

We cannot talk about obedience, and particularly the obedience of Jesus, without thinking of the obedience of Mary. As we end our reflections, let us ask her to dispose our hearts to receive obedience as a gift, a totally free gift coming to us from the Father in the Son, a gift that brings us life. Mary, you who believed all that was said of you by the Lord, teach us how to receive humbly this gift of obedience, and to let ourselves be transformed by it. Amen.

29

Contemplative Chastity

[handwritten margin notes: Tenderness & Respect; Contemplative prayer makes Marriage rich: Respect & awe in each other]

Mary's attitude before God – waiting, availability and receptivity to God's grace, awareness that the supreme end is grace and grace alone – is something that should live in every Christian as a permanent disposition.

[handwritten margin note: Jesus says the way up to dawn]

The Christian does not bring about his salvation by his own strength. He does not build a Tower of Babel by which, developing his potential progressively and accumulating his resources, he tries to reach heaven. Having marshalled all the forces the earth has to offer and having done his very best, he must admit that he is only a poor beggar, a worthless servant. That which truly and finally counts, he must receive from God and from God alone, by pure grace. For what God gives is himself, through love, and no one can merit that. At this level, poverty and virginity express the same thing. Only the barren woman can give birth to Christ, the one who has given up all hope of fecundity. *(Mary is w/o power in her society).*

[handwritten margin note: MT: the (Husband) of Mary / Change in language]

Every Christian must have the ability to give up the world's goods, not only when the world is sinful, trivial and dark, but even when it is beautiful, precious and joyful; an ability to renounce because one believes, in a really concrete way, that God surpasses all created reality and that all created reality has no value except in relation to him.

It is the charism of some of the Church to concretize that in a tangible way of life, in the renunciation of what is most beautiful and nearest to the human heart. They go beyond, and like Mary, make clear that they only receive the unexpected blessing of salvation from grace alone, from on high. The only gratuitousness possible for the poor, for the essentially poor before God that we are, is the gratuitousness of pure receptivity to his love, an availability of our whole being, body and soul, to receive, in praise and joy, the incredible gift of God himself.

Surrender and joy in the pure receptivity of an absolutely gratuitous love, shaping our deepest being and transforming our heart of flesh in Christ into a heart that can finally love: this is the attitude that should mould our prayer. A chaste prayer is poor, with hands open to receive everything, empty hands that do not close over the gift. 'For the Mighty One has done great things for me' (Luke 1:49). It is the Lord who does great things in the depths of our humility. Let us allow him to do them. Why interpose our chatter in the work of the Spirit? Only the Spirit is chaste, because only the Spirit is Love.

It is upsetting to see men and women held back on the threshold of a deeper prayer* by the very riches of the prayer they have built and acquired with so much good will. They possess it and yet are also possessed by it. They are not able to let go of what they think they have; they dread it to the depths in their very flesh; they dread surrendering themselves for good to that fountain of living water that their faith tells them is in them, but which is hidden to the eyes of their human introspection. The scaffolding was necessary to build the spiritual edifice, but now we must get rid of it. It was necessary to clear the wellhead of the soil that covered it over; now let us allow the water to well up from the buried, hidden spring. We are called to be perfect like the Father, to love like Christ, to the point of loving our enemies, even to the gift of our life. That can only be to the extent that we say yes, *fiat*, to the Love that is welling up in us, to the extent that we allow it to well up in our hearts.

We can only be chaste with God's chastity. God is chaste in the totality of his gift of self. In the Blessed Trinity, in the Father, love is total gift; it is total receptivity in the Son, total and fruitful communion in the Spirit. By grace, in Christ, we

---

*It is sometimes, perhaps, the sign of a femininity that has not yet attained its full maturity, or of a sexuality, in the broad sense, that has not been entirely assumed.

Love is its own reward. (handwritten)

Love upon Love. (handwritten, top right)

(handwritten left margin) *Follow the way of the wound of your heart your way*

(handwritten left margin) *Oh Happy Wound!*

(handwritten left margin) *Evil Satan cannot get into our soul.*

are plunged into that river of love. As adoptive sons, the love of the Spirit carries us towards the Father.

The encounter that love desires, between God and me, involves my whole being. Its rendezvous will be the truth, communion between my true self and the true God. But who am I? I enter into the deep caverns of my spirit in order to discover myself and then to be able to give myself. I encounter my demons, the dark forces that dwell in me. I name some of them, but they are legion. I try to determine my interior face, but it dissolves into a thousand changing masks. I want to offer my heart, but my freedom shows itself host to innumerable determinisms, the majority of which elude me. So, am I only the ephemeral confluence of impersonal and obscure forces?

No, even if all the 'matter' of my being were such, my spirit can look at it from outside and say yes or no to it. Seeing what little light I have, I can trust in the light that comes from God and receive from his word the ultimate knowledge of myself. So I know, in faith, that I am made in the image of God, a subject endowed with freedom, called by God to a communion of love, son of the Father in the Son, by the gift of the Spirit. It is the Spirit alone who can tell me my name in the silence of my heart. So let me be silent in prayer in order to hear who I am. My chastity is humble attention before the mystery that dwells in me, that transcends me.

And you, the true God? You alone can say my name. As for me, I must let your word break all the idols I have untiringly built in my own image – the tyrant who frightens, the senile grandfather, the primeval mother in whom I am dissolved, law without mercy, the just employer who rewards my merits, etc.

Only the Son, given up unto death, reveals you as Father, as the One whose essence is to give life through pure love. But that love is so dazzling for my poor eyes that only the eyes of the spirit can contemplate it and recognize it. I abandon myself to them in order to see, without seeing, beyond every image and every word, the incomprehensible glory of your love in the silence of adoration and praise. So I am immersed in your solitude, there where you are in your truth yourself, eternally unique. But since all subsist in you, and you are all in all, your solitude is the place in which all created beings are in communion among themselves. In you, I find them all, and I love them in their truth; I beget them in your love.

Those are the dimensions of our prayer revealed to us by faith. The humble humanity of our distracted and often superficial prayer, our fleeting feelings and our poor words, our wavering desire, our imperfect silence, should not make us deaf to the murmur of the Spirit who prays in us with an ineffable prayer that infallibly reaches God's heart. Let us not quench it; let us allow Prayer to turn us into prayer. The Spirit breathes in us, and the stars shine and sing out their joy.

IMAGES OF CONTEMPLATIVE CHASTITY

Freshness.
Virgin snow.
A ray of morning sun across the shadow of the sanctuary.
A prayer, clothed with a very simple melody.
The song of the stars.
Infinite space.
Light.
Magdalen's tears.
Limpid water.
A mother feeding her child at the breast.
Another's bread.
A cheerful nun.
A joyful cascade.
A child's gaze.
Blue sky.
A flower's mute adoration.
Depth of eyes that love.
A trusting smile.
Gentle rain on every face.
Mercy.
Simplicity of heart.
An old stove in summer idleness.
A worn floor, offered to the feet of all comers, invisible.
Cut stone, single, defenceless.

Open hands that are able to receive without closing on the
    gift and to give gratuitously.
Be.
Peace of the grass.
Smoke from burning wood in the autumn.
A flame.
To be a flame.
Foreigner, only one of his kind.
Solitude.
The silence of expectation.
You.
Mortal wound.
Golgotha.
Father, forgive them!
Pierced and open heart.
Water and blood.
The Body of Christ.
Priest of the sacrifice.
The splendour of the dawn.

V

Work and Contemplative Prayer

My Work is the Lord

The fundamental occupation of the dweller in cell is the Lord. Just as the one Word of God comes to us in the multiple words of human authors, each of whom has his own emphasis and personality, likewise the one occupation of the monk, the *unum necessarium*, takes concrete form in diverse spiritual, intellectual and material activities. The one musical motif is repeated and developed differently on the various instruments of the orchestra. The monk is a man of unity: unity of being, unity of action. This unity develops when everything in him is ordered towards the one goal of purity of heart and, thus, of love. Everything that leaves that axis is fruitless, however useful and fine it may appear to be.

Love is full of vitality. Either it acts or it does not exist. It tends with all its strength towards the Lord: towards justice, truth and love. It uses all the means at its disposal, however humble they may be. Already, faith has enabled the monk to enter into a union with God such as he is in himself. At times, also, love finds in it delight and repose, but then only to be driven more ardently towards the fullness of that union, towards the face of God. All contemplative life consists in a continual swing between these two poles, desire and union.

Contemplative repose is not inertia, the cessation of all activity. Repose forms part of the movement of a whole life, whose most exquisite fruit it is. In our present condition, it can only have limited duration. It needs to be prepared, supported and enclosed within what the monastic fathers called the active life, that is to say, all the activity of body and soul that makes this repose possible. Silence is the plenitude of the word; but if there were nothing but silence . . . So let us accept the humbleness of our human condition and the reality of our sojourn in the land of faith, dissimilarity and distance. We are no angels; therefore let us go to the Lord in the truth of our nature.

WORK IN THE BIBLE

'The Lord took the man and put him in the garden of Eden to till it and keep it' (Genesis 2:15). By forming man in his image, the Lord wished to make him a partner in his creative plan; after creating the universe, he gave it over to man with the power to fill and subdue it (1:28). Man's activity is the fulfilment, the blossoming of God's creation. It is a law of the human condition, and a must for every man.

Yet it is not the whole of man; man is not just his work. 'In six days the Lord made heaven and earth, the sea, and all that is in them, but rested the seventh day; therefore the Lord blessed the sabbath day [*shabat* in Hebrew means repose] and consecrated it' (Exodus 20:11). The activity of creation ends in contemplation ('God saw everything that he had made, and indeed, it was very good' Genesis 1:31) and in repose, which sanctifies creation and manifests its purpose.

Because work is a fundamental fact of human existence, it is immediately and profoundly affected by sin:

> Cursed is the ground because of you; in toil you shall eat of it all the days of your life; thorns and thistles it shall bring forth for you; and you shall eat the plants of the field. By the sweat of your face you shall eat bread until you return to the ground, for out of it you were taken. (Genesis 3:17–19 NRSV)

So the painful side of work has a religious meaning. The early monks were very sensitive to that and assumed it in a spirit of penance, as an instrument of humility. The monk, Christ's poor man, must bear the burden of painful effort and let himself be purified by that ascesis. This is all the more true in that man's work is not just brought to bear on objects outside himself, but also, and more and more so in the modern world, on his own nature and personality, profoundly marked by the scars of sins. The grace of salvation does not dispense man from work, but renders it fruitful.

WORK IN THE GOSPEL

The Gospel's most eloquent pronouncement on work is the humble, laborious life of Jesus the carpenter, and his realistic appreciation of the everyday activities of human life. However, the Gospels only use the word 'work' to indicate the works to which we must apply ourselves, and they are those of God. 'Do not work for the food that perishes, but for the food that endures for eternal life, which the Son of Man will give you' (John 6:27).

Jesus comes to bring us the Kingdom of God. That is what we must seek first of all: 'the Kingdom of God and his righteousness, and all these things will be given to you as well' (Matthew 6:33). 'Your heavenly Father knows that you need all these things' (Matthew 6:32). Christ gives as an example the birds of the air 'who neither sow nor reap', and the lilies of the field 'who neither toil nor spin' (Matthew 6:28). To eat, drink and clothe oneself has its importance; but he who concerns himself with it to the extent of losing the Kingdom has lost everything, even if he has gained the whole world (Luke 9:25). It is a question of proportion: before the absolute of eternal life, all the rest is quite relative.

> Let those who mourn be as though they were not mourning, and those who rejoice as though they were not rejoicing, and those who buy as though they had no possessions, and those who deal with the world as though they had no dealings with it. For the present form of this world is passing away. (1 Corinthians 7:30–31 NRSV)

'*Solis inhiandum aeternis,*' in the words of Guigo ('Only desire the eternal!').

To put work in its place is by no means to devalue it. Precisely by bringing the Kingdom and by revealing our vocation as adopted children of God, Christ shows the whole dignity of

man, and of the work which is at his service. He gives work the
dimensions of charity and brotherhood that should inspire
the Christian in all his activity. Man's progressive domination
of the universe, the impregnation of human relations by justice
and love, mysteriously prepare and begin to realize the Parousia
of the Lord and the fullness of the Kingdom. Creation 'itself
will be set free from its bondage to decay and will obtain the
freedom of the glory of the children of God' (Romans 8:21).

The Lord, My Rock

My eyes are ever toward the Lord,
  for he will pluck my feet out of the net.
Turn to me and be gracious to me,
  for I am lonely and afflicted.

(Psalm 25:15–16)

To you, O Lord, I lift up my soul,
O my God, in you I trust;
  do not let me be put to shame.

(Psalm 25:1–2)

The Lord is my rock, my fortress.

(Psalm 18:2)

These texts admirably express what should be the goal of monastic stability. The monk tends to make of his whole life one continual prayer (3.2). Our heart should be like 'a living altar from which there constantly ascends before God pure prayer, with which all our acts should be imbued' (4.11).

Here I would like to quote at some length from the Conferences of Cassian. This passage gives a good description of the state of prayer towards which we should tend.

If we too want to pray to God with a pure and virgin heart, let us, like Christ, flee the fever and confusion of the crowds, so as to reproduce already in this life some image, at least, of the blessed state promised to the saints of eternity, so that the word of the Apostle: 'God is all in all', may be realized in us.

It is then that we will see the full realization of the prayer our Lord made to his Father for his disciples: 'So that the love with which you have loved me may be in them, and they in us'; 'That they may all be one. As you, Father, are in me and I am in you, may they also be one in us!' The perfect love with which 'God first loved us' will pass into our heart by virtue of that prayer which our faith tells us could not be in vain. And these will be the signs of its presence. There will no longer be in us any love, desire, ardour or effort, no longer any thought, life, word or even breath except for God. The unity that exists at present, of the Father with the Son, and of the Son with the Father, will be communicated to us in our inmost soul. And just as God loves us with a charity that is true and pure and does not die, so will we be united to him through the indissoluble unity of an unfailing love; so attached will we be to him, that we will have no breath or intelligence or word except for him.

We will arrive thus at the goal we have stated, which the Lord also wishes for us in his prayer: 'So that they may be one, as we are one, I in them and you in me, that they may become completely one'; 'Father, I desire that those also, whom you have given me, may be with me where I am'.

Such should be the solitary's goal towards which his whole being should tend: to be worthy to possess already in this life an image of future beatitude, and to have a foretaste, in his mortal body, of the life and glory of heaven. Such is, I say, the goal of the perfect life: that, free and light, the soul should so rise from the carnal regions towards the heights of the spirit, that all its life and movement should become one single, uninterrupted prayer. (Conference 10, 6)

Perfect prayer is the love of God himself communicated to our inmost heart, a love which is always present and entire, uniting the Father and the Son, and uniting us among ourselves. Animated by that prayer-love, we become one, we become monks. That is our goal.

Yet, it is not enough to be enthusiastic about it: we must take the means to realize it, means in accord with our condition as incarnate and sinful beings. Certainly, the very fact of entering a monastery represents the choice of a life's direction, of a form of life totally oriented towards perfect charity. Solitude, silence, the sacramental life, monastic observance, help us and strengthen us. Here, though, I would like to study in greater depth the more personal means at our disposal to assure that stability of the innermost heart in God which permits us to love him with all our heart, all our soul and all our mind. I would like to be as practical as possible. For that reason, let us look first at the life of the Brothers, where certain things appear more clearly.

THE PRESENCE OF GOD

> The aim of the brother's life is, above all else, that, united with Christ, he may abide in his love; hence, whether in the solitude of cell, or in the midst of his work, aided by the grace of his vocation, he should strive wholeheartedly to have at all times his mind on God. (15.18)

The essential practice that should run through all the brother's activities is that of having his mind at all times on God. The monk is someone who is wide awake, who tries to live consciously in the presence of God. The heart that loves turns naturally towards the Beloved.

But do our hearts love God alone? Alas! We love loads of things, we covet a multitude of objects, big and small. Our attention is ceaselessly attracted by the most varied thoughts and images. The young monk discovers that his is a vagabond and rebellious spirit, tossed here and there like a leaf in the wind. A fly dislodges the thought of Christ in his prayer. While he works, it is an almost uninterrupted cinema of the past, of what he could have or should have done, of good or bad desires, of emotions and feelings ... If, by chance, more than by his own doing, a supernatural thought presents itself, he is powerless to retain it firmly for any length of time. What is to be done?

PURITY OF HEART

Continual prayer is not possible without the purity of a heart relieved of its egoism and passionate inclinations. There is work to be done! We cannot hope to live in communion with Christ without the thorough renunciation of everything that separates us from him: sin first of all, but also things good in themselves which claim too much of our attention (for example, a too human curiosity, hyperactivity, an excessive preoccupation with ourselves). We need a great simplicity of heart, a purity of mind (33.3) to live our vocation truly and 'remain hidden in the shelter of the Lord's presence' (6.4).

Such a phrase will resonate in each one according to his grace. No one has ever seen God. He is inaccessible light which cannot be contemplated this side of the grave. However, that light has shone on the face of Christ. To reveal God's secret? Rather, to immerse us in his mystery, all the more incomprehensible in that it pronounces its name in death: love. To remain hidden in that secret is to live in that love and of that love, in adoration, in the silence of God beyond all words, and even beyond all revelation in so far as it is expressed in words. To be engendered by love, to be a son of God's silence. Hidden from oneself and, perhaps, from God?

Let us return to practical questions. What can we do to cultivate the presence of God in our wandering mind?

WORK

The practice of obedience, which takes concrete form above all in work, already achieves the conformity of the will to that of God. This is the basic union with the Lord, the most fundamental of all. Yet the monk would like to be more than a servant of the Lord; he would like to be his friend, bearing him in his heart and in his mind. For this end, work is a precious aid.

'The very weight of our work acts as a sort of anchor to the ebb and flow of our thought, thus enabling our heart to remain fixed on God without mental fatigue' (5.3).

That is true in so far as the work is not too absorbing or done in an agitated manner. A certain interior freedom with relation to work is necessary, a freedom that has to be won again and again for certain temperaments. We should not be totally and uncontrollably drawn out of ourselves. A conscious effort to turn towards the Lord is necessary until it becomes a deep-rooted habit. This should not detract from the seriousness of a job well done and of being ready to serve even in unforeseen circumstances. Work also brings with it the benefits of an enhanced human equilibrium, humility, detachment, and the exercise of an effective charity.

'Interior recollection during work will lead a brother to contemplation; to attain this recollection it is always permissible while working to have recourse to short and, so to speak, ejaculatory prayers, and even sometimes to interrupt the work for a brief prayer' (15.10).

The affirmation is strong: the effort of recollection will lead the Brother to contemplation which is essentially a simple gaze of love towards the Lord. It is not the same thing as thinking explicitly of God. It is something simpler, more encompassing, which happens in the depths of the heart. It is perfectly compatible with activity, at least for those who are practised in it.

The shortest way to reach it is not necessarily to do advanced studies. Study, too, can and ought to prepare the heart; each one has his grace. But there is no direct continuity between the effort of reason and the grace of contemplation. A certain purification of the intellect's functioning and a certain knowledge of the basic truths of the spiritual life are necessary for everyone. The correct amount is a matter of vocation, whether Father or Brother, and of one's personal grace. Nevertheless, to attain contemplation, said St Teresa of Avila: 'The essential thing is not to think a great deal, but to love a great deal' (*Interior Castle*).

IN THE CELL

The impetus of the heart needs to be nurtured and life in cell provides the opportunity.

> Here, they remain quietly and without noise, as far as possible, and follow with faithfulness the order of the day, doing everything in the presence of God and in the name of Our Lord Jesus Christ, through him giving thanks to God the Father. Here (in cell) they occupy themselves usefully in reading or meditation ... especially on Sacred Scripture, the food of the soul ... or, in the measure possible, they give themselves to prayer. (12.3)

In his cell, the Brother should live under God's gaze. He nourishes his soul with *lectio divina*, above all by reading the Word of God. The Word is received into his heart as a germ of light and love. It brings forth its fruit in prayer, intimate communion with the Lord, in his cell or during his work, where the seed slowly sprouts; it has the form of a subject for reflection, or of hidden sustenance for a love that manifests its vitality through short bursts of prayer to God.

THE PRAYER OF THE HEART

In practice, one can retain or repeat some verse drawn from the morning's reading or from the liturgy, ruminate on it or make a repeated prayer of it. Or indeed, one can prefer the greater intensity of a short prayer, always the same, as for example, the Jesus Prayer: 'Lord Jesus Christ, Son of God, have pity on me (or on us) a sinner (sinners)', or simply 'Jesus' or 'Father', etc. This practice is as old as the monastic life itself, and offers a very direct way of turning continually towards the Lord, and of keeping ourselves from forgetting his presence.

To be serious, this prayer requires an alert attention and much vigilance to exclude the bad or idle thoughts and images that present themselves, as well as a certain union of heart and mind, that is to say, a loving gaze, or a love permeated with understanding. The organ of this prayer is the heart. The dis-

cursive activity of the mind is kept very limited, in favour of a
simple but all-embracing movement of the heart. The continual
remembrance of the name of Jesus entails the personal presence
of the Lord, welcomed in a spirit of love and adoration. Nature,
people, and all creation seen and experienced through the name
of Jesus are 'Christified', to so speak, and assumed into the
divinity of Christ.

HABITUAL STATE OF THE HEART

It is worthwhile to recall here a fundamental principle concerning prayer. We will be such at the moment of prayer (i.e. the
moments consecrated to prayer) as we have been during the day,
dissipated or recollected as the case may be. Once again, let us
listen to Cassian on this subject.

> Since you ask me to return to it, I will briefly state the
> means of anchoring our heart.
>   Three things focus a dissipated mind: vigils, meditation
> and prayer; attentiveness and continual application to these
> three exercises establishes the soul in an unshakeable stead-
> fastness. Nonetheless, this is not acquired unless one still
> devotes oneself to steady work, not out of greed, but for the
> sacred needs of the monastery; for that is the means of
> freeing oneself from the anxieties and worries of the present
> life, and of making it possible to fulfil the Apostle's precept:
> 'Pray without ceasing'.
>   He who only prays when he is on his knees, prays little.
> But he who, on his knees, yields to every distraction, does
> not pray at all. So, before prayer, we must enter into the
> frame of mind we wish to have during prayer; for it is an
> inescapable law that the dispositions of the soul depend on
> the state that preceded it; and we will see it either rise
> to the heights of heaven or sink to the earth, following its
> previous thoughts. (Conference 10.14)

32

Work as Contemplation

Work is a contemplative act. Union with the will of the Father in all the works inspired by obedience is the inexhaustible nourishment of one who hungers for God.

All the activities which are necessary in order that the community may live become, for hearts enlightened by faith, a sacrament of Jesus the worker, a communion renewed without ceasing with his person and his life on earth.

For one who has received the grace, an occupation of the body and hands easily becomes as it were an anchor, allowing the heart to remain fixed on God, and to remain present to that love which calls to him in the silence of the workshop. To the mind which is never at rest, short ejaculatory prayers or a familiar interior dialogue keep living that presence of the Word, always near to us as a friend. Finally, the redeeming and purifying value of work, even the hardest and most trying, gives us the possibility of letting shine the paschal light in our hearts and on the world, at the price of sharing in the cross of the Saviour. So work is, of itself, a prayer in various ways, with which God is pleased, providing we accomplish it with a good will, according to our talents.

It is likewise a direct preparation for those hours more specially consecrated to liturgical praise or to interior silence in the recollection of the cell. Human stability and that sense of responsibility which it helps to maintain are the support for the flowering of an authentic supernatural relation with God, under dependence to the Holy Spirit.

Again, those inevitable cares and difficulties we meet when assuring that our work is going well keep us in an attitude of confident dependence on the Father and sustain a humble prayer of petition.

Our work is a service. We do not give ourselves up to it for our personal interests, or to dominate, but to allow ourselves to be transformed into the likeness of Christ who came to serve.

From this point of view, we are responsible for a real service to the Church. Every service rendered in union with Jesus bears fruit as if it were accomplished by the Lord himself. More precisely, permitting our brethren of the cloister or the lay monks to lead their life of solitary prayer is to give to the Spouse of Christ those true adorers she needs to respond to the ardent seeking by the Father.

Serving necessarily implies a great forgetfulness of self, if we desire to give to each one in love that which he really needs: without seeking to care too much for one's own rest, one's own strict timetable, and sometimes even those hours of personal prayer in the cell, in order that we may respond to the needs of charity or of obedience.

It is at once a consolation and a help to think that our service becomes, by God's will, an indispensable condition for the existence of our monasteries. Our work must never be limited to the role of a mere relaxation. It is a joy to find ourselves one with the poor, and to impose on ourselves a minimum of daily work, so that the activity of our service always keeps an important place in our daily life.

'My father is working still, and I am working' (John 5:17).

33

Work – Help or Hindrance?

In the following paragraphs we will use the term 'work' for simplicity's sake; but in most cases, the same observations apply to the activities other than work that occupy us outside the times reserved for prayer.

The value of work with respect to prayer depends very much on the attitude we bring to it. Work is a human reality willed by God, and has intrinsic value, if we accomplish it with all good will. Apart from the intention with which we do it, it has been explicitly willed for us by the Lord: 'The Lord God took man and set him in the garden of Eden to till it and keep it' (Genesis 2:15). We have to acknowledge, however, that in certain cases the work, if it is done conscientiously, is not compatible with prayer, or that the actual dispositions of the monk make it impossible for his work to be effectively a prayer. Prayer and work will then be juxtaposed, and not directly related.

We can be faced with several possibilities:
– work is an aid to prayer,
– work seems to be neutral with regard to prayer,
– work is actually an obstacle to prayer.

DIRECTING ALL OUR OCCUPATIONS TO THE SERVICE OF CONTEMPLATION*

Experience proves that certain occupations are *indirectly an aid to prayer*. If we carry them out in the appropriate conditions of

*1.5.1.

peace, purity of heart and recollection, they are the stock, as it were, on which prayer can be grafted.

'Human labour, by fostering a happy equilibrium between mind and body, helps the brothers to profit more from solitude' (2.15.2). Monks have long known that giving free vent to a certain need for activity, tiring out the body, and applying one's attention to an object other than prayer, far from being an obstacle to prayer, is actually an aid to recollection. The bow-string cannot remain continually taut. So, from this point of view, there is no doubt that work has a positive value, even if it is a source of distraction while we are actually doing it. But we must emphasize the importance of the conditions we mentioned above, for if they are not fulfilled, work will become a source of distraction or restlessness during prayer.

Other occupations, on the contrary, can immediately influence prayer, which will intensify as we continue our work. 'It sometimes happens that the very weight of our work acts as a sort of anchor to the ebb and flow of our thought, thus enabling our heart to remain fixed on God without mental fatigue' (1.5.2). This is very beautifully expressed, and the reality is not always equal to it; but it certainly points us in the right direction. It is an ancient tradition, of which we find traces in the Fathers of the Desert, and which corresponds to normal psychological balance: focusing the surface of our attention and giving the body some little thing to do frees the mind and allows it to turn gently, and without effort, to God. In this matter, as in all else, we need practice, and the beginner will sometimes need to be trained by an elder, more experienced than himself. Often we have to learn how to 'work'.

Finally, our work can be the beginning of a *dialogue with God*. It is a way of turning lovingly to God, in a simple exchange between the monk who is at grips with creation and the Lord who has entrusted him with this work. We have a fine example of this in the Statutes (cf. 2.15.18) when it is said that, for the brother in charge of the infirmary, the sick are an image of Christ in his sufferings, and a call to find him there. Guigo's 'Meditations' are full of examples which show how the little details of life inspired him to raise his heart to God.

Look at the thorn bush: it starts here in one spot, then spreads out branches and takes root everywhere. So it is in your soul, where love fixes its roots in countless clods of earth, clinging to them with unrelenting tenacity. It also clings to the sentiments and favor of others, and is dependent on them.*

There is no set rule for this kind of prayer that arises spontaneously from our work: it is up to each individual to discover within the seeds of prayer the Lord has planted there and make them sprout and fructify. We need attention and perseverance so as not to be overcome by the passion for work and the satisfaction we draw from it, forgetting that the Lord is transparently present in it.

WORK AND PRAYER JUXTAPOSED

'One day when I was engaged in manual work, I had started thinking about man's spiritual activity, when suddenly four spiritual degrees were offered to my reflection' (Guigo II, *Ladder of Monks*, Letter on the contemplative life). Guigo's observation introduces us to a form of prayer that is relatively frequent: whilst our hands set to work on some task, our mind takes flight at liberty, with hardly a thought for what the body is doing. Work and prayer go their own ways, with little influence on each other.

After Guigo, the Statutes too refer to this form of prayer during work: 'It is always permissible while working to have recourse to short and, so to speak, ejaculatory prayers, and even sometimes to interrupt the work for a brief prayer' (2.15.10). Our work is not the mainstay of our prayer; on the contrary, it is even envisaged that we can interrupt our work in order to regain the minimum of liberty we need to fix our mind on God.

Here we may meet with a difficulty: our attention can be torn between God and our work. It is not easy to keep our minds fixed simultaneously on the Lord and on the details of

*Section 372, *Sources Chrétiennes*, Vol. 308.

the work at hand. When this difficulty arises, are we not going
to feel increasingly tense, and our prayer end by being a source
of fatigue rather than a rest in God? 'No one can serve two
masters' (Luke 16:13).

Is it not because we set off on the wrong track that we have
this difficulty? Unless a human mind is exceptionally gifted, it
cannot normally engage in several activities simultaneously for
any length of time. We have to choose. In this case we have to
give priority to the work, which is God's will for us. Do we
therefore have to renounce prayer? (while working)

St Augustine gives us the answer:

> Your desire is in itself your prayer, and if your desire is
> continual, so also is your prayer. It is not in vain that the
> Apostle says: 'Pray without ceasing'. Do we have to be
> always kneeling down, prostrating or raising our hands,
> since he said: 'Pray without ceasing'? . . . If you do not want
> to cease praying, do not let your desire cease: your continual
> desire is like a continual voice within you. It is only when
> you cease loving that you become silent . . . When charity
> grows cold, the heart becomes silent; the flame of charity is
> the cry of the heart. If charity abides, so does prayer. (St
> Augustine, on Psalm 37[38])

But let us be quite clear: we would not be satisfied if we
simply said: 'I am doing my work to please God so it is a
prayer'. This point of view is not false, but it is not enough.
We want more. During our work, we try to 'allow the Holy
Spirit to lead us into *the depths of our heart*' (1.3.2). This
expression drawn directly from the Statutes points to the solution. In order to go to God, we do not need the discursive
activity of our intelligence or the effort of our minds. In certain
activities, these are indeed necessary to keep our attention fixed
on what we are doing. But an encounter with God takes place
in the heart, and our heart can 'stay awake' while the rest of
us is occupied with our work (1.5.5).

This distinction between heart and mind is sometimes quite
revealing, with regard to the way we see people and objects: we
are accustomed to an approach which is too logical or too
rational. But the standing summons to the heart of man to turn

to God plunges its roots into the earliest monastic traditions, and above all into the Bible. It is not a feature of some particular culture, but a fact of experience founded on human nature. We have too often forgotten this in our Western way of thinking, and we must be among the first to rediscover it: our search for God can then be sustained in a deep and natural way, without the exhausting and disappointing efforts we impose upon ourselves.

We have many indications of this in the Statutes. This is not the place to give a detailed commentary, but we can touch on certain aspects. Already Guigo, in his appreciation of Mary's sitting at the feet of the Lord and listening to him in silence, gives us this description of her attitude: 'She purifies her spirit, prays in the depths of her heart, and seeks to hear what God may speak within her' (1.3.9). The place of prayer is the heart; and we said earlier that the aim 'of our patience, and of our assiduous meditation of the Scriptures, is to introduce us, by the grace of the Holy Spirit, into the depths of our heart: there we can not only serve God, but also cleave to him in love' (1.3.2).

These directives orient us towards the centre of ourselves, where we are open to 'a tranquil listening' once our mind has been purified and is calm and silent (1.4.2). This is the aim of life, for 'God has led us into solitude to speak to our heart' (1.4.11). And in this sense, as we said above, work is sometimes a source of recollection for our mind, allowing 'our heart to remain fixed in God' (1.5.3).

These brief comments suggest a path to be explored for remaining united to God in all circumstances, in a tender, intimate way, without having to do ourselves violence. For it is 'to the heart that the Lord speaks' when he comes to us.

WORK AS AN OBSTACLE TO PRAYER

We come now to the main reason for the present discourse: it has often been said, a bit cynically, that it is impossible to lead a real contemplative life in the Charterhouse because work is an obstacle to prayer. There are brothers who wonder what real difference there is between their lives and the life of a good working man. There are Fathers who refuse to work, because it would tear them away from pure contemplation. Have we not all experienced days on which we feel completely disoriented after a period of work, once it is time to take up our prayer again?

Does the difficulty come from the work itself? Usually not, if it is carried out under the conditions of recollection, silence and separation from the world, envisaged by the Statutes. If it so happened that certain kinds of work were, by their very nature, a source of distraction, then we would have to ask ourselves if it were acceptable for us to keep doing them.

Yet, in most cases this is not the problem. It lies in ourselves. We do not know how to approach our work with the right attitude of mind and heart. One of the first explanations for work's being an obstacle to prayer is the carelessness with which we go about it, with no regard for proper organization. *If* the laws of nature are violated, and *if* in what we do, we do not take account of the relative value of objects, or the successive stages of a task, it is not surprising that, sooner or later, we are faced with a revolt: we will be abnormally worried about our work, tired out of all proportion and unreasonably overwhelmed with distractions.

We will not be lacking in the spirit of prayer, but, rather, fostering it, if we take the time to reflect calmly on our work, in order to approach it and accomplish it in an intelligent way. The brothers are invited by the Statutes to 'apply their natural powers and gifts of grace to the work committed to them' (2.15.3). Also, the Procurator and the Heads of Obediences* are requested readily to consult those in their charge and give them a hearing (2.15.4). This recourse to our gifts of nature, in order to make a better use of them, and in view of a greater development of all our human capacities, is the foundation on which grace can act.

The Statutes speak of this wisdom with regard to obedience,

---

*An 'Obedience' in the language of the Order is a post committed to a brother's care, whether it be kitchen, carpenter shop, bakehouse, laundry, machine shop, etc.

but how much more is it true with regard to prayer. This touches an important point concerning the quality of our prayer, and which goes far beyond the confines of work. If nature is not properly ordered, it cannot be the foundation on which we build a life of recollection, and more especially, times of prayer totally turned to God. Because of our interior unity as persons, when we come to prayer we bring with us inevitably, although perhaps unknowingly, all the disquiet that we have imposed on ourselves during the preceding hours or days. If we have not beforehand tried to keep our heart or our body in a state of order, truth and beauty, we cannot expect them to be suddenly transformed, just because we shut our eyes and want to be in the presence of God.

The quality of our prayer is a function of the way we live throughout the day. If there is wisdom and order in our approach towards the whole rhythm of our daily activities – our sleep, the way we take our meals, the times of rest – then these will be the remote preparation for our recollection during the times specially set apart for prayer. 'On hearing of the inflexible rigour of your ordered observance . . . my spirit rejoices in the Lord,' writes St Bruno to his sons at the Charterhouse. May we deserve the same praise.

There is another reason, linked to the previous one, that our work becomes an obstacle to the prayer which should accompany or follow it: we do not approach it with sufficient purity of heart. Here again we enter an area in which our work is only one aspect of a much wider question: the one of *monastic asceticism*, which must impregnate our whole existence if we want to advance continually towards God, and be ever preparing ourselves to meet him.

We have to admit that we often become slaves to work because we renounce all custody of our heart. We engage passionately in whatever it is we are doing. We allow this to become our real centre of interest. On this point, let us recall a very forceful passage of Cassian. Even if it is only at the end of a long spiritual journey that we can reach the stages he describes, the orientation he gives us is always valid, and we must continually return to it:

> If we are to pray with the necessary fervour and purity, the
> following discipline must be carefully observed. First, you
> must completely surpass all the anxieties of the flesh . . .
> renounce all unkind and empty talk, gossip and clowning.
> Above all, you must entirely expel the emotions of anger
> and sadness; you must uproot the noxious seedlings of sen-
> sual desire and the spirit of possessiveness. All such vices,
> that are visible even to our fellow men, must be cut away and
> destroyed. But after this preliminary work of purification has
> received its crown of innocent simplicity and purity, the
> foundations must be laid: unshakeable foundations of a *deep
> humility*, capable of bearing the tower that is to rise even to
> the heavens . . . (Cassian, Conference 9.3)

Cassian gives us here a complete programme of monastic life.
If, only too often, our work disperses us, it is because we are
not honest and resolute enough in our efforts to maintain a
monastic attitude with regard to it. We forget that 'our whole
life is ordered to uniting us with Christ and abiding in his love'
(2.15.10). It is certainly an austere task, requiring sustained
efforts; but if we accept the challenge, it will become a particularly effective form of asceticism for us, and, by the purification
it imposes on us, will lead us to God. The Statutes are saying
exactly this when they recall that 'ancient monastic tradition
assures us that work contributes greatly to the practice of those
virtues from which flows perfect love' (2.15.2).

VI

Liturgy

34

Ebb and Flow*

THE LITURGY: END AND SOURCE

The liturgy is at once both the end to which the action of the Church tends and at the same time the source from which flows all her strength. We who have left everything to seek God alone and to possess him more fully, should carry out the liturgical functions with particular reverence. For when we accomplish the liturgy, especially the eucharistic celebration, we have access to the Father through his Son, the Word Incarnate who suffered and was glorified, in the outpouring of the Holy Spirit. Thus we achieve communion with the Most Holy Trinity.

A SIGN OF CONTEMPLATION

When we celebrate the divine worship in choir, or recite the Office in cell, it is the prayer of the Church which is being offered by our lips; for the prayer of Christ is one, and through the sacred liturgy, this one prayer is wholly present in each member. But among solitary monks, liturgical acts manifest in a special way the nature of the Church in which the human is directed and subjected to the divine, the visible to the invisible, action to contemplation.

---

*6.41.1–4.

A COMPLEMENT TO SOLITARY PRAYER

Throughout the centuries, our Fathers have taken care that our rite should remain suited to our eremitical vocation and the smallness of our communities, by being simple and sober and ordered primarily to the union of the soul with God. For we know that Mother Church has always approved of a diversity of liturgical rites by which her catholic and undivided nature is all the more clearly manifested. Thus, through the sacred rites, we are able to express the deeper aspirations of the Spirit, and prayer, springing from the depths of the heart, when it finds an echo in the sacred words of the liturgy, acquires a new perfection.

LITURGY PERFECTED BY SOLITARY PRAYER

Again, communal prayer, which we make our own through the liturgical action, is carried over into solitary prayer by which we offer to God an intimate sacrifice of praise, transcending all words. For the solitude of the cell is the place where a soul, enamoured of silence, and forgetful of human cares, becomes a sharer in the fullness of the mystery by which Christ crucified, rising from the dead, returns to the bosom of the Father. A monk, therefore, provided he strives continually to cling to God, exemplifies within himself what is signified by the entire liturgy.

35

Heaven, Earth and the Depths of the Heart*

> **Behold a great multitude standing before the throne and before the Lamb and crying out with a loud voice.**
>
> **(Revelation 7:9–10)**

Dear Fathers and Brothers,

In today's Mass we read one of those texts of Revelation that describes the impressive scene of the multitude that no one can number, singing with loud voices the glory of God Most High, around the throne and the Lamb. The density and richness of John's vision are such that words seem hardly able to express it; for it signifies not only the eschatological prayer of the saints, when all will finally have been gathered into unity, but also the present prayer of the Angels and the blessed in heaven, and the prayer of the Church here on earth journeying towards that unfailing light.

The feast of All Saints should enkindle in us the desire to participate even now, and as fully as possible, in this liturgy which unites heaven and earth in a common praise of the Lamb, and of the Father. Today then, let us try to understand a little better the link uniting our solitary prayer, the prayer of the Church, and the eternal prayer of the blessed in heaven.

---

*Sermon preached on the Feast of All Saints.

We think of prayer first of all as a return to our inner world. Is not turning to the Lord first of all a matter of being recollected, of entering into the silence of our cell and shutting out exterior noises, entering into ourselves and remaining there, listening to God's intimate word to us? This is the constant teaching of the ancient monks, and all those who wanted to live a deep Christian life, and it cannot be denied. Does this mean then that solitude closes us in on ourselves, and cuts us off from others? The seduction of being wrapped up in oneself, and simply contemplating one's own self is no vain temptation for a solitary. It is indeed quite possible to lose real solitude and fall into isolation, to enter into this inner world only to enclose oneself there in an ivory tower: but this is no longer prayer; it is, on the contrary, a renunciation of real prayer. St Bruno tells us that entering into deep solitude means acquiring that clear gaze which wounds the Bridegroom with love; it is a meeting with someone, a descent into one's inner being that is so deep that self is left behind, in order to be open to God, and to establish a relationship of love with him.

This is the deep reality of my prayer: it is not my lifelong effort to be recollected, and to apply myself to meditation, but meeting the tenderly loving gaze of God resting upon me. This is the permanent, unchanging substance of my prayer; this is the spring of water welling up into eternal life, to which I am continually returning to drink. Beyond all I can see, hear and feel, is the light of the divine Face shining down on me. So, far from enclosing me in a narrow, limited interior world, prayer draws me completely out of my own self. Under the gaze of God, I am placed in his world, and welcomed into the midst of the communion of the Father and of the Son in the Spirit. But under this gaze, I am also incorporated into a wholeness in which I am not alone: in the light of the Spirit I discover that I am the stone of an edifice. When I pray, inevitably I will feel that I have to relate to every other stone in the edifice, and I will know myself to be in intimate solidarity with the whole which lives in me and in which I live. However, the full reality of our prayer is more than this. For the only objective of the Spirit who prays within us is to bring to life in us the reality of all that Jesus has given us. Jesus, the Son, is in fact, and forever, the very substance of our turning to God; he immolated himself for us and with us, in order to bring us into the bosom of the Father. This is what cements our unity, and is the palpable reality of our prayer: the bread that we break together and the cup that we share, his body and his blood. This indeed is what constitutes the plenitude of our prayer. It is something which englobes us completely, body and soul: the fine point of the spirit as well as the visible weight of the flesh, the deepest silence of the soul, and the tender movings of the heart. We are taken over completely, to be assumed into the unity of a renewed humanity, which constitutes the new creation, unified and transformed in the Lamb who is seated on the throne of God for eternity.

These are the perspectives of Revelation. Every prayer is a participation in the hymn of glory sung by this renewed humanity, that is, by the Church: 'Amen! Blessing and glory, wisdom and thanksgiving, honour, power and might be to our God for ever and ever! Amen!' (Revelation 7:12). Every prayer, even the most secret one, even the one which is the least expressed in explicit words – every prayer is an activity of the Church; it is the very life of the Church which is turned towards God in incessant praise and adoration; it is the continual birth of the Church receiving her being from God, thanking him for it, presenting the needs of all her children to him with unwavering trust.

This does not mean that every time we pray we have to conjure up these splendid visions; it simply means that our interior silence is filled with a reality which transcends it infinitely, and which cannot be expressed in human words.

And yet, even here on earth there is a prayer which does express all this: it is the holy liturgy. The liturgy is the visible, sacramental reality of the prayer of the Church. It exists first of all, and fundamentally, in the community at prayer, in the actual, living community to which we belong. We experience it every day in choir, and in the intimacy of our cell, as well, when we are reciting the Hours of the liturgy in union with our brothers, or when celebrating the Eucharist in a chapel on our own. These are the times when all that we have been speaking of becomes a visible reality, an actualization, as it were, at our level, of the truth of the Body of Christ, drawing humanity to God through our voice and the prayer of our heart. But this liturgy of our own community is also the prayer of the Catholic Church. Spread over the whole world, in communion with Peter, this Church gathers together in the same faith and a common love, the hearts of all those who are nourished with the same bread, because they are living by the same Spirit. Our prayer then, having these dimensions, reaches to the extremities of heaven and earth; and the immense multitude of Christians living in the whole world merges into one with the innumerable hosts of John's vision. Here we see realized the new Canticle that is sung to the Lamb:

> Worthy are you to receive the scroll and to break open its seals, for you were slain and with your blood you purchased for God souls from every tribe and tongue and people and nation. You made them a kingdom and priests for our God, and they will reign on earth. (Revelation 5:9–10)

At this point we can no longer draw a line between exterior and interior prayer. Praise of the lips and recollection of the heart are fused, and complementary. We can affirm with equal certainty that the exterior prayer of the Church is the fruit of the secret action of the Spirit, and that, on the other hand, in the silence of solitude there is a celebration of a liturgy of the heart. The latter is the interior, secret aspect of the mystery of the liturgy, without which the prayer of the Church would only be pretence. The aim of our life is to establish a unity between the official liturgy and this liturgy of the heart. In the words of the Statutes, they are in continuity one with the other; they are inseparable, for there is, in reality, only one prayer; the prayer that is presented before the throne of the Lamb.

We still have one more aspect of prayer to consider. We have looked at its interiority, and at its incarnate expression in the community or Church; but today's feast makes us look further. The liturgy, even here on earth, is the beginning of a new reality, and of a praise that will continue for all eternity. For the prayer of the Church is not a static, immobile attitude, but movement and life, and it is continually going forward. Prayer is not hanging on to what we already possess, but starting off on the way towards something we thirst after without yet knowing it, something which we know is there awaiting us, even though we cannot yet see its form clearly. It is the visionary of Revelation again who says:

> Then I saw a new heaven and a new earth. The former heaven and the former earth had passed away, and the sea was no more. I also saw the holy city, a new Jerusalem, coming down out of heaven from God, prepared as a bride adorned for her husband. (Revelation 21:1-2)

The liturgy is the manifestation in our life of our constant awaiting of the blessed day when we will see this new universe appear. In a way, we have nothing else to do here below but to be the vigilant servants, waiting for the return of their master. Waiting in the night, we are certain that the bridegroom will come back from the wedding; we know that he is already on the way to meet us; we are sure he will arrive at any minute. And we are waiting. Our waiting is filled with certitude, and our vigilance is in some sort already rewarded, for he has promised us he will return soon. Is not this what is signified by the long psalms that we recite, side by side, during the hours of the night, and that keep us alert? We are not gathered there together to learn about something new, but simply to keep alive in our hearts the flame of this unceasing vigil.

What is the source of this perseverance that never seems to wear out? It certainly does not come from our personal strength, nor from any conviction of our own making. It comes from our knowing that the reality to which we are tending already exists. Eschatology, this new and definitive world, is not just a reality for tomorrow. It already exists in Jesus. It is becoming a reality now, at this very moment, in the glorious passage of Jesus from this world to his Father that the liturgy is celebrating and actualizing, everywhere where the body and blood of the Lord are offered, and in every place where the Church is singing before the throne, in union with the angels, the twenty-four elders, and the four living creatures. Yes, we are waiting, and yet, at the same time, in a hidden way, we are already in possession of the reality. 'Christ is risen'; and each day the victory of Easter shines through the simple fact of our being gathered together around Christ, and in him, in such a way that a part of ourselves is already hidden with him in God.

We cannot end this meditation without speaking of Mary, who is already, and for all time, the perfect realization of the prayer of the Church. She is the Bride whom the Bridegroom receives and presents before the throne. She is the one who offers her glorious Son to the Father; she is the new creature in whom our eyes can see the universe transformed into glory. She is the one who brings us to birth, because her prayer is continually answered. Above all the united praises of Angels and men together, the song of the Virgin Mary is the most precious of praises that can ascend to God. When she is silent, the elders bow down to adore, and the four living creatures repeat unceasingly: 'Amen!'

36

The Monk as Priest

The Christian, every Christian, by the very fact of his baptism, is a priest inasmuch as he shares in the priesthood of Christ, that is, inasmuch as he shares in the risen humanity of Christ in the Spirit, and as his being and whole life are transformed by it. We should find there the same features as in Christ.

The Christian is a priest as man, in all the dimensions of his humanity and every aspect of his nature; that is, not only in his soul, but in his body as well, and in his heart. For good or ill, he is one with his brothers, all his brothers.

The Christian is a priest as a son of God, born again in the water of baptism and by the gift of the Spirit, and already raised to life in Christ by faith. As son, he enters into the movement of Christ towards the Father by opening himself to him and allowing himself to be transformed by the Spirit implanted in the depth of his heart, where he prays: 'Abba, Father'. As son, he is able to 'do his service to the living God' (Hebrews 9:14), a sacrifice of praise, a song or silent adoration, not only a ritual activity (this has its place) but his whole life transformed by the priestly love of Christ.

This love is shown:

First, by his filial obedience to God in the total gift of self, the placing of his whole human existence at the disposal of the Father for the glory of God and the salvation of his brothers.

Second, by his openness towards his brothers, his solidarity with them, lived in compassion, prayer, intercession, mutual help: consumed, offered for them, offered to them, in the Spirit.

Third, by his entry into intimacy with the Father with the confidence of a son who knows himself to be welcomed unconditionally, and loved for his own sake.

All this applies to every Christian, called by the very fact of his baptism to realize in his life this sharing in the priesthood of Christ which we call the common priesthood. Monastic life can be understood as a way of living this priesthood.

THE MONK

The monk has no other consecration but that of the Spirit, no other transformation but that of the Son. The monk only employs more radical means of realizing in his whole life his status as son.

The features which characterize the monk are: unity, universality, eternity, just as in Christ, just as in the Christian. Here we are at the point of intersection of the Christian, the monastic and the priestly lives, both common and ministerial. The monastic life can be thought of as a priestly reality in its totality – in the sense of life as wholly transformed by the priestly love of Christ. The ministerial priesthood exists to serve that end.

UNITY

The monk is one, at least in name and intention. He is a man who has chosen a single aim – the love of God and neighbour. In addition, he has chosen a very definite manner of life where all is ordered as directly as possible towards this end, whence a great simplicity, unity and vitality.

Even as the offering of the Christian is his whole existence directed towards God, so the monk, in so far as he achieves this in actual fact in his heart and life, approaches the unity revealed in Christ between what is offered and the one who makes the offering. Ancient tradition has seen a certain appropriateness in the monk's becoming, thus unified, the instrument whereby Christ makes present sacramentally in time his eternal and unique love-sacrifice. This explains the priestly ordination of solitaries who have rarely exercised their ministry, or even in certain cases, rarely celebrated the Eucharist. This is the eremitic priesthood described from the historical point of view by Dom Jean Leclercq.

Every monk will have experienced the singular and irrepressible movement in which his life, his whole being, are enfolded each time he offers Christ to the Father.

UNIVERSALITY

Separated from all, yet one with all, the monk – above all the solitary – has need of broad perspectives. His gaze, released from the constraints of limited tasks, tends to range ever more widely. His heart yearns to become as boundless as the heart of Christ, to embrace all men, without distinction. In this respect, the monk rejoins the prayer of the priest, which is primarily concerned with the whole of mankind. The particular intentions which the priest may have when celebrating Mass are not the principal object of his eucharistic intercession. For certain Carthusians, this universal openness is very important and is lived intensely. Compassion, intercession, presence, communion, praise – these are his very heartbeat.

ETERNITY

The risen Christ has entered into the glory of God. He has brought there his whole humanity and all mankind. Our transitory and inconstant efforts are founded on the rock of his eternal sacrifice, eternally offered. Our faltering prayer is rooted in the prayer of him who is always heard 'because of his submission' (Hebrews 5) – because of his filial love. The Father always hears us, for the Son's voice is identical with his own.

Our contemplation, for all its obscurity, is nonetheless a sharing in the face to face contemplation of Christ and his Father, in the eternal love that is the Spirit. The only difference lies in the hidden nature of our faith on earth. We enter truly into the glory of God; we know him as he is in himself; we love him with his own love.

The monk is urgently called to enter into the intimacy of the

Father. This is the life of prayer. The man of the desert, in particular, is invited to pass through the true tent and enter into the Holy of Holies; there, no idol is allowed and the Divine Glory is enthroned in all its mystery and majesty.

In the temple of Jerusalem, there was firstly the vestibule, then the tent and lastly the inner sanctuary, the Holy of Holies. To reach the latter, one had to pass through the two others. The tent recalls the Tent of Meeting which Moses set up in the wilderness, according to what he had seen of God's dwelling place when he met God on the mountain. The Jerusalem temple was modelled on the Tent of Meeting. Both are but material images of the Divine Glory, the uncreated Glory of the Father.

We are called to enter the true Sanctuary, beyond every image, every representation, through the true tent of meeting with God. This tent is the glorified body of Christ.

> Christ has come, as the high priest of all the blessings which were to come. He has passed through the greater, the more perfect tent, which is better than the one made by men's hands because it is not of this created order [it is the body of the glorified Christ]; and he has entered the sanctuary once and for all, taking with him not the blood of goats and bull calves but his own blood, having won an eternal redemption for us. (Hebrews 9:11–12 JB)

Let us recall the Jewish liturgy of Yom Kippur ('Day of Atonement' or 'Great Pardon') in which the High Priest, unaccompanied, made his entry into the sanctuary of the temple to sprinkle the mercy-seat, the place of the Lord's unseen presence, with the blood of two victims previously sacrificed. This ritual was the definitive act to which the expiation of sins was attached. For the author of the Letter to the Hebrews, this corresponds to the Ascension of Christ, his entry into heaven, which is thus considered the culminating point of the mystery of salvation.

It is perhaps at this point that the way of the monk and that of the priest meet at the deepest level. The Christian priest, in Christ, enters into the divine Glory as it truly is in itself, through the body of the glorified Christ perpetually immolated, represented in a sacramental manner. The monk – man of the desert and of prayer, man of the prayer of the desert, often man of the desert of prayer – seeks for his part also to enter into the true Glory of the Father, beyond every image, every symbol, in a proximity of offering and acceptance as total as possible. Moreover, the living way which he follows is the same. It is that of the mystery of Christ, his death, Resurrection and Ascension genuinely lived in his human nature – true death, truly risen life, transforming a human body and heart in the fire of the Spirit.

Prayer is offering, consecration, holocaust, communion. The desert is the no-place of Mystery, the plunge into the beyond. The tent of meeting is the prayer of our fervent beginnings; the temple made by human hands is the edifice of our desire, our perception of God, our good will. The temple is only a copy, the place of the multiple and ineffective (Hebrews 9:24).

To enter the true sanctuary, we must die to 'our' prayer, we must pass through a tent *not* of man's making, not of this creation. We have to receive from God the way through, made available in the humanity of the glorified Christ and communicated to us in the sacrament of faith. We have to receive the prayer of Christ by being transformed through his death into his risen state – a condition realized in our life and in our whole being. In this way, we shall have access, in the spirit, to the face of the Father, to his intimacy, his Glory, radically other, yet radically close.

Tradition speaks of a fitting union between the priesthood and the monastic state: the Mystery of Christ, Victim and Priest, realized in one and the same person, in a special way.

The grace of the ministerial priesthood sets on every priest the stamp of Christ the priest, and tends to liken him to the Lord. The priest-monk presents no specifically new feature. It is a question of a different way (the Mystery is or should be realized firstly in one's special life, then in the sacrament), and of a particular emphasis upon certain aspects of priesthood because of the actual circumstances of its exercise (little or no pastoral ministry). One of those aspects, in my opinion, is the plunge of adoration in the silence of the Mystery of God. Another would be a love wholly open in radical poverty, arms outstretched over the whole human race, all given in simple abandonment. Perhaps, too, transparence of life, in the joy of living, something of the radiance of the risen humanity of Christ the Priest.

Here, too, could be found the Christian roots of a cosmic priesthood which enables the universe to sing praise and adoration in all its created splendour. The solitary, above all, cannot leave the earth and the heavens to be without voice for God.

Finally, the awaiting of the full realization of salvation, nourished by the sacramental memorial, is lived intensely at the heart of a prayer wholly directed towards the light invisible, and refreshed by a hidden water which serves only to revive his thirst for love.

Maranatha! Come, Lord Jesus!

Conclusion

37

Separated from All, United to All*

What benefit, what divine delight, solitude and the silence of the hermitage bring to those who love them, only those who have experienced them can tell. Yet, in choosing this, the best part, it is not our advantage alone that we have in view; in embracing a hidden life we do not abandon the great family of our fellow men; on the contrary, by devoting ourselves exclusively to God we exercise a special function in the Church, where things seen are ordered to things unseen, exterior activity to contemplation.

If therefore we are truly living in union with God, our minds and hearts, far from becoming shut in on themselves, open up to embrace the whole universe and the mystery of Christ that saves it. Apart from all, to all we are united, so that it is in the name of all that we stand before the living God. This continual effort to be always – as far as human frailty permits – very close to God, unites us in a special way with the Blessed Virgin Mary, whom we are accustomed to call the Mother in particular of all Carthusians.

Making him who is, the exclusive centre of our lives through our Profession, we testify to a world, excessively absorbed in earthly things, that there is no God but him. Our life clearly shows that something of the joys of heaven is present already here below; it prefigures our risen state and anticipates in a manner the final renewal of the world.

By penance, moreover, we have our part in the saving work of Christ, who redeemed the human race from the oppressive bondage of sin, above all by pouring forth prayer to the Father,

*34.1–5.

and by offering himself to him in sacrifice. Thus it comes about that we, too, even though we abstain from exterior activity, exercise nevertheless an apostolate of a very high order, since we strive to follow Christ in this, the inmost heart of his saving task.

Wherefore, in praise of God – for which the hermit Order of Carthusians was founded in a special way – let us dedicate ourselves to the peace and silence of our cells and strive to offer him unceasing worship, so that, sanctified in truth, we may be those true worshippers whom the Father seeks.

Epilogue

The Poor Communities*

Montalegre: eleven monks. Only eight, if the sick aren't counted. I was Procurator for seventeen years and have been Prior for two.

For a long time there has been talk of closing Montalegre. There are no vocations.

This has created discouragement, anxiety and a certain guilt. It is like a sword of Damocles.

We must try to get beyond this situation and give it some meaning. In the Gospel I have found light. I do not recall any place where Jesus assures us prosperity and success in this life. Rather the reverse: the strait gate, the narrow way, contempt, the Cross. The Gospel asks us to follow Jesus in his poverty.

So I thought about our poverty of numbers and quality also, the lack of resources and our uncertain future. And I discovered that our situation is almost ideal for living the Gospel, not in theory or as an asceticism, but quite simply in living from day to day. Thus I came to confidence in God, but a confidence that for the most part is blind, without any light or sensible consolation, but accompanied by sorrow.

The words of Jesus have come alive for me: 'The Father cares for you.' 'Seek first the kingdom of God and the rest will be added unto you.' 'Sufficient unto the day is the evil thereof.' Above all the passage where the apostles' boat is foundering in the storm. A real tempest, not an imaginary one. Jesus is asleep. And when he wakes he reproaches the apostles for their lack of faith. Thus we have to have confidence and above all when everything apparent says we shouldn't. This is the paradox of the Gospel.

Paradox of the Gospel

Manifesto presented to the General Chapter by the poorer communities, 1993.

In reality, I am myself of this mind, disposed towards an absolute trust, almost to the point of absurdity, perhaps the absurdity of the cross.

But can I lead the community in this direction? Perhaps I am trying to justify the situation, or ease my mind, or delude myself. Anything is possible. But, even so, I will have confidence in God and I believe this is right. God deserves this blind trust, and, I repeat, it is almost always sorrowful.

Perhaps the danger for the poor community is a deeper impoverishment at the level of aspiration (a little like the underdeveloped countries): a certain conformity or resignation in the face of reality; a regret for the past; obsession with vocations.

But we learn to simplify the life, better to seek what is essential: God and our neighbour; to prize fraternal charity more than rules or norms. And finally, whatever happens, to accept the will of God. Fiat!

* * *
*   *

*   ***O Bonitas!***   *